NEUROPHYSIOLOGICAL INSIGHTS
INTO TEACHING

NEUROPHYSIOLOGICAL INSIGHTS

INTO TEACHING

A Report on
Reading, Writing, and Spelling Disabilities
and
Discussion of the Interrelated Use of
the Sensory-Motor Avenues—
An Integrated Approach to Teaching

By

Marion Fenwick Stuart

PACIFIC BOOKS, Publishers
Palo Alto, California

First printing January 1963
Second printing June 1963
Third printing June 1964
Fourth printing October 1965
Fifth printing June 1966
Sixth printing April 1967
Seventh printing July 1969

Pacific Books, Publishers
Palo Alto, California

PREFACES

Views of an Educator

This is a book about children and how they learn and about teachers and what they do to insure that children learn. Yet this is not just another how-to-do-it book on the subject of teaching methods. It is, rather, a how-and-why-to-do-it book.

The book begins with some brief pictures of children who have specific language difficulties in reading, writing, and spelling and then proceeds to trace both the psychological and physiological problems which are involved in the enormously complicated task of learning.

Education has long been in need of a treatise on teaching which links the art of teaching with the science of the study of the human organism. Marion Stuart has attempted to make such an approach in her presentation of methods of teaching, which deal specifically with children who have language difficulties and with classroom teaching in general.

The basic methodology suggested is sound. First, study the child, with particular reference to understanding how he learns. Second, develop hypotheses of how to present material which will be meaningful and which will result in a learning experience. Third, apply this tentative method. Fourth, evaluate the outcome. The teacher who follows the teaching which is here explicated will find a new meaning in the medical report on the child, in the psychologist's report on the child, and even in the value of the everyday opportunity to observe how children receive stimuli and react to them.

Miss Stuart has examined what might be called a neurophysiological approach to understanding the learning behavior of children. While many of the applications here presented deal with children who have been found to have specific language difficulties, the methodology and indeed many of the findings and suggestions apply with equal meaning to any children. Miss Stuart suggests with some force that teachers may have placed too great a reliance on the eyes and the ears, that learning actually involves activating not only the eyes and ears, but also speech, touch, and motion in simultaneous and in highly interrelated ways.

Beyond this section on the child as an organism, or what some doctors have called "the skin and all its contents," Miss Stuart investigates and reports briefly on experimental methods of teaching which have been developed both in America and in other places. Again, the experimental studies, the findings, the principles, apply in the teaching of all children.

The teacher who follows through with this general concept of the teaching-learning process will find that every day's teaching is indeed a new experience, that teaching every child is a unique experience. The teacher here described will find that research is bound up closely with the daily task of teaching, will find that the task of the teacher is to take the hypotheses and suggestions which come from primary research, test them for applicability in the classroom situation, and carry through with the next step in the process--the developmental step, the application of the research hypothesis to the classroom learning situation.

This process has been closely identified with the development of American industry in what is known as the research and development plant. Education has had no parallel to this intervening variable—the development agency. Much of psychological and educational research lies dormant in libraries because it has been developed with a small sample in a particular situation and is perceived as not applying to the classroom. Yet what is needed is the second step—the "D" component of the R and D plant.

Miss Stuart has had opportunity in her unusual setting of working with individuals and groups of children in a situation which gave opportunity for experimenting with many methods, to pool some of these learning and teaching hypotheses from a vast array of research studies, and to try them out in her classroom situation.

Education is anchored to science—the application of objective methodology to the development of principles of teaching and learning. Yet teaching is an art. The reader will find that this book about teaching does not read like a laboratory manual. It presents a dedicated teacher working with children. Amid all the documentation, the footnotes on research, there emerges the picture of a warm, sensitive teacher vitally interested in the outcomes of the teaching process for every child. Teaching could not be otherwise.

Henry Bonner McDaniel, Ph.D.
Professor of Education and Psychology
Stanford University

Views of a Physician

For several years educators and parents have been plagued by the fact that many bright children experience relatively great difficulty in learning language skills. At the present time, our feeling that all our available brain power must be realized has resulted in an extraordinary emphasis on education. Consequently, it has become doubly important to explore the problem of poor reading and spelling, and to seek methods of solving it.

Miss Stuart's book makes a unique contribution in this field. In the first place she goes beyond the usual and proper assumptions that learning to read and to spell well are dependent upon adequate vision, hearing, intelligence, motivation, and teaching. She stresses the variations which may also exist in the way different individuals' brains function and the consequent differences in the ways they learn. It is important that this fact be emphasized, and she has done it with great clarity and simplicity, taking the mystery out of the neurological approach to learning, and culling the relevant and the valid from those reports of research which frequently are both inaccessible and couched in forbidding language and which, at all events, have too often been ignored. Furthermore, she compels the reader of her book to renew a pledge to take a more thoughtful and understanding look at any child who fails, and to resolve never to explain away his difficulty with a cliché and never to attempt to correct it without due regard for the question of what method of teaching is likely to be best suited not only to his feelings and his intelligence, but also to his brain. Even in our democracy we need constantly to be reminded that each of us has individual differences, and that no one method of teaching, no matter how expertly employed, can be the most effective for all.

For those young people of good intelligence who exhibit an ability to learn mathematics and science, but who fail miserably unless the initial efforts to teach them to read and spell employ the sorts of principles implicit in the alphabetic-phonetic approach--and for the country which will lose their services unless they are spared the failure and the frustration and antagonistic attitudes which follow teaching methods inappropriate for them--Miss Stuart has rendered a particularly valuable service.

The understanding teacher who will apply the points of view and the principles the writer has so clearly stated--that teacher will multiply the value of this book's contribution many times.

J. Roswell Gallagher, M.D.
Chief, The Adolescent Unit,
The Children's Hospital Medical Center,
Boston, Mass., and
Lecturer on Pediatrics,
Harvard Medical School

ACKNOWLEDGMENTS

For twenty years I have been working at the application of the substance of this book. The content has grown out of my teaching along with reading, studying, listening, and discussion with scores of parents and professional persons. The valued contributions from these personal encounters and from books, merged with the knowledge and experience given me by hundreds of my pupils, have become so much a part of me in both philosophy and practice that I scarcely know how to make a complete acknowledgment.

It is my earnest hope, in citing documentation, or sources of documentation which I believe to be of value to readers, that there remains no inaccuracy or oversight. I have made every effort to be scrupulously careful to acknowledge ideas and materials initiated by others. Any errors of fact or interpretation are my responsibility.

As for the actual accomplishment of this book, obviously I could not have succeeded without drawing upon the labors and experience of many experts. Consequently, I speak of the following persons with thanks:

Henry Bonner McDaniel, Professor of Psychology and Education, Stanford University, served as my adviser. He gave me direction and encouragement; he maintained confidence in my purposes, and showed great patience for what has been a long-term production.

Dorothea Walker, writer, Ojai, California; Lois Walsh, teacher, Palo Alto Senior High School; and the late Helena Van Courtlandt Smith, remedial specialist, provided keen personal interest in the cause delineated in this manuscript. They spent hours of faithful effort in helping me not only with ideas, but also with revision of composition and placement of content. My debt to them is great.

Physicians who gave generous help were: J. Roswell Gallagher, The Children's Hospital Medical Center, Boston; Walter Friedlander, Veterans Administration, Boston; and Bruce Jessup and Muriel Bagshaw, Stanford Medical School.

Among the many persons who have helped without being aware of their usefulness to my manuscript the following should be mentioned: Charles Abildgaard, Children's Memorial Hospital, Chicago; Ernest Hilgard, Pauline Sears, Robert S. Turner, all of Stanford University;

Elizabeth Addoms, New York University; Cecilia Brinton, Cambridge, Massachusetts; and Signora Emma Pampiglione, Rome, Italy.

Those who assisted in the way of testing, advising, explaining, or demonstrating include: Jean Turner Goins, North St. Paul, Minnesota; June K. McFee, Stanford University, Stanford, California; E. J. Anderson, Wayland Public Schools, Wayland, Massachusetts; Reta V. Buchan, The Children's Hospital Medical Center, Boston; Robert Filbin and staff members, Lincoln Public Schools, Lincoln, Massachusetts; Katrina de Hirsch, Pediatric Language Disorder Clinic, Columbia-Presbyterian Medical Center, New York; Mildred Plunkett, Massachusetts General Hospital, Boston; Mary Helen Robinson, Atherton, California; Stanley Croonquist, Palo Alto, California; Florence Chu, Stanford University Library, Stanford, California; Georgina Fenwick and Margaret Girdner, both of San Francisco, California; Barbara Hadley, Norwalk, California; Barbara McAndrew, Ross, California; Jesse M. Phillips, Menlo Park, California; Freya Owen, Palo Alto, California; and Geneva Torrey, Lincoln, Massachusetts.

Teacher specialists who contributed were: Edna Andriano, Los Altos, California; Marymary French, Felton, California; Paul Engelcke, Cramer Owen, Jewell Teale, Craig Vittetoe, of the Palo Alto school system; and Dorothy Ketman, formerly of the same system.

A fellow teacher who made the music photographs was Dorothea Hardy; original chart drawings were prepared by Joe Chew and Reginald Walsh; chart lettering was done by Lewis Kiracofe; and photostating was managed by Chris D. Stevens—all of Palo Alto, California.

Secretaries in Palo Alto, California, were Lois Winkelhake whose consummate skill solved many problems; and Peg Bogert and Shirley Hanan who helped willingly with extra work. Ruth Mersereau, The Children's Hospital Medical Center, Boston, facilitated my work in the East.

Inspired educators whose writings have been an unending resource for practical ideas and a vision of possibilities were Anna Gillingham, Grace Fernald, and Maria Montessori.

And finally, Winfield Christiansen and Dwain McCleary, principals, Palo Alto school system, have given unstinting support; Lois Kingham and Maude Arnold, colleagues, have experimented with me willingly; the children have guided me into a greater understanding of the learning process; and my family, of course, has expended years of belief in my efforts.

Marion Fenwick Stuart

Palo Alto, California
July, 1962

TABLE OF CONTENTS

INTRODUCTION

The main aims in the preparation of this book are to center attention on a noteworthy ten per cent or more of our children with average or better than average intelligence who have specific language disability in reading, spelling, and writing; and to explain and discuss an organic or neurophysiological approach for all teaching.

As pointed out in the Prefaces, the book is not essentially a step-by-step, how-to-do-it book. What I have done is to make known the nature of the need for a neurophysiological approach, and to gather together sources which will be helpful in making needed application and experimentation. Although examples and some application of method are included, an urgent consideration has been to build for teachers a background in this approach, and to make plain its significance for teaching and for learning.

My major purposes are listed in rather formal style, but it is felt that, as the reader proceeds, the purposes might be useful for reference in this form:

A. To identify and define the language problems of a particular segment of intelligent children--those with specific language disability (S.L.D.)--and to report on useful teaching techniques.

B. To examine and present a teaching approach which integrates pertinent neurophysiological and psychological principles of learning.

C. To demonstrate that these principles have value not only for children with specific language disability, but also for other children in the regular classroom, and for any subject.

D. To emphasize the indications that sensory-motor avenues used simultaneously or in other interrelationships result in better learning for all students.

E. To make available—within the covers of one book—resource material from medical, psychological, and educational research which has timely application for teaching. That is to say, to present a synthesis of usable research.

F. To encourage and urge teachers and teacher-training institutions to use the material and the original sources introduced here, and to work experimentally with a neurophysiological approach. (At present, in our country, some experimentation is in progress, but much should be undertaken.)

The term "neurophysiological approach" may sound theoretical, but as used here it means activating eyes, ears, speech, touch, and motion in a simultaneous or in an interrelated way to establish concepts for objects, for words and their parts, or for ideas. It concerns the integration of the parts and the whole.

This process of building and strengthening associations by providing these close intersensory and motor relationships suggests many varied opportunities for making learning experiences meaningful to children. Consequently, the exploration that follows is one which considers aspects of our constitutional organization—how different the mental functioning of one intelligent human being is from that of another, and how this difference in function affects teaching procedures. It probes beyond method and delves into principles that should embody method.

Since it is my intent to work out the plan in logical sequence, a few remarks about each chapter should be of use here.

Chapter One emphasizes the medical point of view on reading, spelling, and writing disabilities which belong in the classification of specific language disability.

Chapter Two is concerned with information from both psychological and medical sources—buttresses for the neurophysiological approach. One of the important results of my years of investigating and teaching in the area of specific language disability is the realization that the principles underlying teaching the child with this difficulty, and even adaptations of some of the methods used, could be useful in the regular classroom. The material in Chapter Two unfolds backgrounds for this idea. For this reason it is placed at this point in the manuscript, between a description of two groups of children—those with specific language disability and those with diverse problems.

Also in Chapter Two there is recognition for the growing acknowledgment of the interconnection between neurophysiology and psychology. Although there will be much reference in this study to the simultaneous and interrelated use of the sensory-motor avenues, this is not to be interpreted as meaning only a robot-like stimulus-association-response activity. As will be indicated, there is basis for believing that within the brain there is a central system of integration—that reading, for instance, is a cerebral function.

Chapters Three and Four have practical suggestions and are written with the neurophysiological approach to teaching in mind.

Chapter Five acquaints the reader with Maria Montessori—great in so many ways—and all but unknown to teachers in the United States today.

Chapter Six summarizes the material briefly and anticipates some questions which will be asked by teachers.

It will be observed that the ideas and research of many persons from a variety of disciplines are assembled in this manuscript. This assemblage, this synthesis of original sources, has been created purposefully. The references selected yield significant insights into teaching—and they make a related whole in providing these insights.

My hope is to develop a point of view by bringing together this documented material in organized form so that teachers and other readers may be encouraged to think in terms of a neurophysiological approach to teaching and to practice the principles involved.

NEUROPHYSIOLOGICAL INSIGHTS
INTO TEACHING

CHAPTER I

THE CHILDREN: PART ONE

Intelligent Children Who Cannot Read and Cannot Spell:
Specific Language Disability

The following letter was written by a fourteen-year-old boy whose intellectual functioning on an individual test placed him in the superior range. At the time this letter was written, he was enjoying his first experience of camping alone. He had set up his own housekeeping in a high mountain campground.

July 24

Hi Mom

I'v Just got theru eating 3 egges scrambeld, $\frac{1}{2}$ can span, 6 slises of french bread, and 2 cups of coffee so I gess you dident by to much.

I hav nice nabers. The man is a teacher in som calage. I just cant get away frum teachers. His wife offerd me some pancake mix after I had alredy eatin so I had to refuse. I have a resolushon im alwes going to eat brecfest after my nabers.

The rangers sune is hear at T---- but hes an a trip right now so I havent seen him yet.

The weather is wonderful up here. I was nice and worm last night and my cote worcked real good at the campfire to.

I'm schedualed for a thre dy hick next week 31, 1, and the 2. The ragers are taching about 15 pepal and 5 muals with all the food. It will cost me $3.00 for the food and muals, and I ges Ill get my monys worth out of the fude for shoor.

Well Im gowing fishing with some boys I met at the capfire so I had beter sine off

Your sone

W--------

The spelling may seem spectacular but the difficulty is not one that he has been able to help. His original, basic problem is that known in medical literature as specific language disability.[1] As defined by one medical authority, it is "a condition characterized by the inability of an individual readily to acquire, and subsequently to use, one or more language skills with a facility commensurate with his intelligence or with his facility in learning science and mathematics, and in addition not commensurate with the opportunities which have previously been offered him to learn. . ." Furthermore, not only is there lack of facility in these skills, but also a tendency to carry out these language activities in an unusual manner; such individuals, for instance, are not only poor spellers-- they often spell in a "bizarre fashion."[2] Reduced to its simplest explanation, it is "the inability, in an otherwise normal, healthy, and intelligent child, to master reading, writing, and spelling as quickly and easily as he masters other subjects. He usually understands arithmetic well, although he is more likely than the others to produce a wrong answer on paper by reversing the order of the digits. (He knows that 3 x 4 is 12, but his fingers put down 21!)"[3]

It would be obvious that the boys about to be described all have, or have had, specific reading and spelling difficulties. Four out of five were in public school. The results of individual intelligence tests were I.Q. scores ranging from 124 to 151. Following a brief description of each boy, there will be a more detailed consideration of the problem.

These children and some of their characteristic language problems are presented (1) to help school people and parents become aware that specific language disability is a particular category of language difficulty,

---

1. Some other names given in the literature for this disability are: word blindness, specific dyslexia, strephosymbolia (twisted symbols).

2. J. Roswell Gallagher, M.D., "Specific Language Disability (Dyslexia)," Clinical Proceedings of the Children's Hospital, Washington, D.C., Vol. XVI, No. 1, Jan., 1960, p. 4.

3. Richard S. Eustis, M.D., "Specific Reading Disability: Information for Parents and Teachers." Originally published in The Independent School Bulletin, the Independent Schools Education Board, Milton, Mass. Series of '47-'48, No. 4, Apr., 1948. Revised, July, 1954, and reproduced for use in The Adolescent Unit of the Children's Medical Center, Boston, Mass.

(2) to spotlight attention on the point that, although the intelligence may be at any level, it is <u>not</u> children of inferior intelligence, but those of average or better intelligence who are ordinarily classified in this category, (3) to stress the need for identification of these children <u>early</u>, preferably, and (4) ultimately, to explain that teaching approaches designed to prevent or correct the problem involve saying, seeing, hearing, and writing all organized in such a way as to build close association and imagery for letters, sounds, syllables, and words.

I will begin with Warren.

Name: Warren R.
Age: 16 (at time of testing)
Grade: 10

The results of the Binet scale showed Warren to excel in ingenuity, mastery of codes, comprehension of concepts, and problem solving and to have difficulty with right-left orientation, sentence memory, and re-arranging dissected sentences. Results of the Differential Aptitude Test placed him in the 99th percentile of abstract reasoning.

He wrote with his right hand, and his mother reported that general right-hand usage had been consistent since babyhood. His big muscle coordination was poor, but eye-hand coordination was superior. In music his sense of rhythm was above average.[4] Although Warren finally learned to read, it was a long, painful process involving school grades repeated and a succession of remedial teachers. At one time he barely escaped placement in an English class for pupils below average ability. Actually, his written expression was sensitive, colorful, and perceptive, but

---

4. According to Stambak, sense of <u>musical</u> rhythm does not develop with age—rather, it is an individual characteristic.

In pursuing the matter of rhythm more comprehensively, however, it will be noted later on that among the characteristics which may be demonstrated in specific language disability is a <u>poor ability</u> to reproduce short rhythm patterns by tapping. Again referring to Stambak, her investigations with rhythm tests showed that there is a strong possible tie-up between a <u>poor</u> sense of time relationships and specific reading disability. Mira Stambak, "Le Problème du Rythme dans le Développment de l'Enfant et dans les Dyslexies D'Evolution," <u>in L'Apprentissage de la Lecture et Ses Troubles—Les Dyslexies D'Evolution</u>, by Zazzo, Ajuriaguerra, and Others, Presses Universitaires de France, Paris, 1952, pp. 480-502.

handicapped by incredible spelling. For example: The ice cave "was just butaful - all the lovely kristals. . ." "It was nuthing to cumper (compare) with anething I have ever seen." ". . . so I sat ther looking back at all the wonders in a pond of ice wotter about 3 in. deap." Performance in written examinations was utterly damaging—with spelling as a contributing factor.

Name: Richard B.

Age: 8-9 (at time of testing)

Grade: 4

Richard tested above his mental age in such matters as finding reasons, copying the bead chain from memory, solving problems of fact, and understanding abstract words. He tested below his mental age in sentence memory, rearranging scrambled sentences, rhyming, and story memory.

It is to be noted that he entered the first grade before he was six years of age.

He was ambidextrous, but used the left hand for writing. There was evidence of spatial confusion; he had done mirror writing in the early grades; and he had poor visual recall for words. He had difficulty, too, in connecting sight of words with sound. Arithmetic answers in column addition and multiplication were frequently transposed.

When he reached the fourth grade, pressures of competition were forcing a breakdown in behavior, health, and morale. Time from his regular class for individual remedial tutoring in reading, spelling, and arithmetic was arranged for Richard.

Name: Bob W.

Age: 10 (at time of testing)

Grade: 5

This gifted boy had very superior reasoning ability, and he passed ingenuity tests at a high level. His use of abstract words and his memory for sentences indicated good language function in certain areas.

One of his major difficulties was with right-left orientation.

Bob had been reading easily for about one year. He tested above grade level in reading, but he had been slow to start, and in the early grades he had been a stutterer. Although he had mastered visual recognition of words (for reading), and although he had auditory memory for words and sentences, he did not have it for the individual speech sounds. He was not connecting sight of words with sounds.

Consequently, his visual imagery for recognition of words was good enough for reading, but not good enough for retention of spelling. This fact, coupled with low auditory imagery for the sounds and syllables in words, made the spelling handicap severe. In addition, there was the confusion over right and left orientation, and handwriting was difficult for him—and poor and cramped in appearance.

Testing results further indicated higher scores for verbal ability than performance; and in arithmetic he was superior.

Naturally, the spelling disability hampered all written expression, and his discouragement over this failure became another factor in his continued failure.

Name: Howard J.
Age: 8
Grade: 3

Howard's strengths lay in his ability for immediate recall, his capacity for rapid understanding, and his ease in assessing practical situations. He was happy during the performance tests, but demonstrated considerable anxiety on tests that required verbal items or those that were reminiscent of school.

He was ambidextrous, using his right hand for throwing and eating, and his left hand for writing. His visual recall for words was poor and the sounds of the phonograms made little impression on him.

By the time Howard reached the eighth grade it was still necessary for him to attend the reading clinic—although he could read and study on his own. His spelling continued to require constant checking. His grades were C's and B's, and it was thought these would be better if it were not for the spelling.

Name: George W.

Age: 8 (at time of testing)

Grade: 2

George's reasoning powers were classed as very superior. Among his strengths were understanding of abstract words, memory for sentences, ability to rhyme, finding reasons, and carrying out a plan of search.

His failures involved memory for repeating digits in reverse order, memory for stories, and putting together scrambled sentences.

The examiner noted that, although George drew with his right hand, he started at the right side of the paper and moved to the left.

When tested, George was reading at about high first-grade level. Although he had ability to rhyme and had memory for sentences, he was having trouble recognizing individual sounds in words. He could spell orally, but had difficulty recalling how to write the words. He was continuing to write reversals of letter sequences and of words. He confused "b" and "d", "p" and "q".

The school questioned the wisdom of promoting him into the third grade, so summer tutoring was planned.

These are the children who mystify their parents and their teachers. A common factor among these five, for example, is that they are all bright. What is holding them back? How can we understand their difficulties? What are the techniques which have been developed to help them? How can the teacher master these techniques?

What Is Specific Language Disability?

Let us continue now with a more detailed consideration of this problem. As a beginning, it is helpful to recall that the term "specific language disability" (S.L.D.) is one used by the medical profession to describe the problems of approximately ten per cent or more of our children of average or better than average intelligence who have specific difficulty in learning how to read and spell, who may have difficulty with handwriting, and who have a problem, too, in mastering foreign languages.[5] Often they do well in mathematics (providing the story problems are read to them) and in science.

It is important to understand that this ten per cent does not refer to children whose difficulties are traceable to poor vision and hearing, to inferior intelligence, poor teaching, poor school attendance, etc., nor does it refer to children whose school problems are primarily emotional in origin. Rather, it refers to children who have difficulty in mastering language symbols.[6]

Among the characteristics[7] which these children may exhibit singly, or in combination in degrees of difficulty varying from mild to extreme, are:

1. Poor visual perception and memory for words

    In spite of normal vision, even after repeated effort, they cannot remember the words they have studied. Recognition is either absent or poor.

    Reproduction of words (spelling) may be phonetic (see letter, page 3) because the visual memory for words is so uncertain.

---

5. J. Roswell Gallagher, M.D., and Herbert I. Harris, M.D., Emotional Problems of Adolescents, Oxford University Press, New York, N.Y., 1958, pp. 141-143.

6. J. Roswell Gallagher, M.D., "Specific Language Disability: A Cause of Scholastic Failure," New England Journal of Medicine, Vol. 242, No. 12, Mar. 23, 1950, pp. 436-440.

7. Hermann makes it clear that although many diverse sorts of errors may be found in "congenital word-blindness" such as the frequency both of rotating letters, and of reversing them in a word, "there are no types of error so characteristic that the diagnosis of word-blindness can be based on them alone." He points out that inexperienced readers and spellers among normal children make some of these same mistakes during their early exposure to reading and spelling, but they overcome them—whereas the word-blind child does not. His difficulty remains long continued and persistent.

Hermann draws attention, too, to the inconsistency of word-blind persons' errors: They "will write a letter character correctly and neatly one moment, but be quite unable to do it the next . . . The same feature is found in their reading . . ."

Knud Hermann, M.D., Reading Disability, Charles C Thomas, Springfield, Ill., 1959, pp. 43, 64 (with permission of the original publisher, Munksgaard A/S, Copenhagen).

2. Poor auditory memory for words or for individual sounds in words

> In spite of normal hearing, short auditory span may show up in speech or spelling, or both. Many cannot distinguish between close gradations of sound.

3. Reversal and confusion in direction

> Right and left confusion may produce reversals of words, syllables, or letters in reading, writing, or speech. Examples are: "was" for "saw," "sowro" for "sorrow," "b" for "d," "p" for "q." (Hermann labels the confusion between letters "rotations" ("b" for "d"), and the reversed sequence of letters and syllables "reversals" ("was" for "saw").[8] Not only may the confusion produce reversals, but also such reversals are usually more numerous and persist much longer than in other persons—far beyond what is considered to be normal learning time.

> Up and down confusion may produce inversion of letters, such as "m" for "w," or "p" for "d".

> Several other possibilities are oral mix-up of whole sentences, mirror writing of sentences, or transposition of numbers.

4. Poor recall for reproduction of simple figures

> On being shown a picture of a simple figure such as the following ——[], there may be inability to recall and reproduce this with any degree of accuracy—after removal of the picture. (A series of pictures is used.)

5. Ambidexterity

> Uncertainty as to which hand is more comfortable to use may continue—a slowness in establishing habitual right- or left-handedness. Or the use of the same hand for the same task may be inconsistent.

6. Clumsiness, poor coordination

> Early clumsiness in learning any gross physical act may be present, and coordination required for achieving finer motor skills, such as game skills, may show up later on as below average. They may, however, perform well in large-muscle sports, such as swimming and football.

7. Poor ability to reproduce rhythm sequences

> Reproducing short rhythm patterns by tapping may be difficult.

---

8. Ibid., pp. 44, 46.

10

8. Speech disorders

Stuttering, lisping, or lack of oral facility with language may be present, or speech development may have been slow.

In addition to the above indications are two more of considerable interest:

1. Hyperactivity

The following refers to case histories studied:

"In reviewing a large number of family histories taken over a period of years, however, we find reports of early hyperkinesis and disorganization in children under eighteen months . . . As a matter of fact, some of the mothers offer the comment that their children have been unusually active even in utero. Many of them show no indication of psychopathology, but their driveness, their difficulty with inhibition of motor and emotional responses, seems to fit in with the rest of their behavior."[9]

2. Perceptual confusion

Weakness in selecting "the figure from the background" may be present. In this particular situation, the printed sentence, as foreground, is not distinguished from background, which is the page. It appears as a scrambled jumble without meaning. "For one to decipher a printed sentence, the configuration must be well defined and sharply delineated against the page."[10]

A belief that disturbance of Gestalt function (see footnote 22) is basic to dyslexia is held by Drew. He presents three cases in one family and suggests that this disturbance of Gestalt function is an inherited dominant trait. "If viewed as defects in Gestalt function many of the reported correlates of reading disability [mirror-writing, reversals, spatial confusions, for example] become comprehensible as parts of a single fundamental defect."[11]

Several additional relevant matters should be noted. First, most of the literature indicates that by far the larger proportion of children with specific language disabilities are boys. "Only about one per cent of girls

9. Katrina de Hirsch, L.C.S.T., "Gestalt Psychology as Applied to Language Disturbances," The Journal of Nervous and Mental Disease, Vol. 120, Nos. 3 and 4, Sept.-Oct., 1954, pp. 258-259.

10. According to de Hirsch, "Weaknesses in figure-ground relationships have not been systematically explored in children with severe reading disabilities." Katrina de Hirsch, "Tests Designed to Discover Potential Reading Difficulties at the Six-Year-Old Level," The American Journal of Orthopsychiatry, Vol. XXVII, No. 3, July, 1957, pp. 570-571.

11. Arthur L. Drew, "A Neurological Appraisal of Familial Congenital Word-Blindness," Brain, Vol. 79, 1956, pp. 457-458.

suffer from this difficulty."[12] "Most nonreaders are males (7 or 8 cases out of 10). It is, therefore, a sex-associated condition."[13]

Second, there is much evidence to indicate that the disability has a hereditary tendency to manifest itself in one or more forms--not necessarily the same form or same combination of forms. Information given by Richard S. Eustis, M.D., to parents and teachers explains that "Specific reading disability, therefore, seems to be merely a part, although the most serious one, of a family tendency toward confusion between right and left, ambidexterity, comparative clumsiness, and relative weakness in the use of language."[14] He believes the evidence supporting this belief is "impressive."[15] [16]

12. J. Roswell Gallagher, M.D., "Can't Spell, Can't Read," Atlantic Monthly, Vol. 181, No. 6, June, 1948, p. 37.

13. Edwin M. Cole, M.D., "Specific Reading Disability: A Problem in Integration and Adaptation," American Journal of Opthalmology, Vol. 34, No. 2, Feb. 1951, p. 230.

14. Richard S. Eustis, M.D., "Specific Reading Disability: Information for Parents and Teachers." Originally published in The Independent School Bulletin, the Independent Schools Education Board, Milton, Mass. Series of '47-'48, No. 4, Apr., 1948. Revised, July, 1954, and reproduced for use in The Adolescent Unit of the Children's Medical Center, Boston, Mass.

15. Citing one example from his own experience, he describes family members of four generations as follows:

"Of thirty-three descendants over 2 years old, fourteen (42 per cent) show one or more of the disabilities. Of twenty-five descendants over 6 years old, twelve (48 per cent) show one or more of the disabilities. Most of these disabilities are comparatively mild.

"Obviously, neither ambidexterity nor left-handedness is any great drawback to a successful life. Unusual bodily clumsiness merely leads to a lack of prowess on the athletic field. Motor speech delay by itself is of no great import, although it frequently precedes defective speech. None of the latter in this series have been severe.

"Specific reading disability, on the other hand, has been a great handicap to the three boys afflicted by it. In the three girls it has been much milder and has responded much more quickly to remedial training." Richard S. Eustis, M.D., "The Primary Etiology of the Specific Language Disabilities," The Journal of Pediatrics, Vol. 31, No. 4, Oct., 1947, p. 449.

16. De Hirsch, too, refers to the study on congenital word blindness by Bertil Hallgren done in Stockholm, Sweden, as follows: He used the Child Guidance Clinic in Stockholm and a secondary school having special classes for "intelligent dyslexic [S.L.D.] children. He investigated all parents and siblings in his group as to past and present performance in reading, writing and spelling. His results were striking: in 88% of his cases one or several members of the immediate family had a history of dyslexia or were still suffering from the same difficulty." Katrina de Hirsch, L.C.S.T., "Specific Dyslexia or Strephosymbolia," Folia Phoniatrica, Vol. 4, No. 4 (1952), p. 235 (published by S. Karger, Basel/New York). The reference for Hallgren's study is as follows: Bertil Hallgren, Specific Dyslexia: Acta Psychiatrica et Neurologica, Supplementum 65, 1, 1950.

For further information on genetic aspects see the investigations done on twins by Edith Norrie discussed in Knud Hermann, Reading Disability, Charles C Thomas, Springfield, Ill., 1959. See also Arthur L. Drew, "A Neurological Appraisal of Familial Congenital Word-Blindness," Brain, Vol. 79, 1956, pp. 440-460.

DOMINANCE

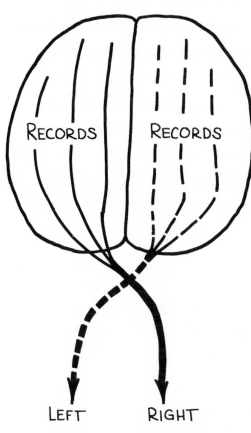

RECORDS | RECORDS

LEFT   RIGHT

See footnote 18, chapter I.

And third, what can be said about the cause of these language problems? There seems not to be total agreement on cause in spite of careful neurological studies.[17]

In our own country, Samuel Torrey Orton formulated the hypothesis that failure to develop dominance of one cerebral hemisphere over the other causes confusions, reversals, and mirror writing.[18] [19]

In Denmark, neurologist Knud Hermann believes that the reading and spelling problems of word-blind people have as their basic, primary cause "an inherited underdevelopment of directional function" (up-down, in-out, forward-backward, right-left, etc.) with the greatest directional

17. "Its basic cause, though still unknown, would seem to be a disturbance in neurological function, but it should be distinguished from neurological disorders which are less amenable to treatment such as those following anoxia [insufficient oxygen] at birth, or following encephalitis [inflammation of the brain], and those resulting from intellectual and sensory deficits, and from learning problems primarily due to emotional disturbances."

J. Roswell Gallagher, M.D., "Specific Language Disability (Dyslexia)," Clinical Proceedings of the Children's Hospital, Washington, D.C., Vol. XVI, No. 1, Jan., 1960, p. 3.

18. Dominance in this situation refers to the dominance of one cerebral hemisphere, or one side of the brain, in controlling language function. Orton's qualifying term is "unilateral cerebral dominance." It is important to understand, too, the counterpart of dominance—that there is relative dominance since the hemispheres are interconnected. "Inasmuch as both cerebral hemispheres have a function in language but that one is far more capable than the other the two may be designated as major and minor." J. M. Nielsen, B.S., M.D., F.A.C.P., Agnosia, Apraxia, Aphasia: Their Value in Cerebral Localization, Paul B. Hoeber, Inc., New York, N.Y., 1948, p. 94.

In relation to dominance, a late experiment in remedial reading, classed as the neuropsychological approach, is reported by Carl H. Delacato, Ed.D., Chestnut Hill Academy, Philadelphia, Penna. This experimental approach sets up a procedure to achieve unilaterality in the child before the remedial reading program

(continued on page 15)

<table>
<tr><td align="center">(a)</td><td align="center">(b)</td><td align="center">(c)</td></tr>
</table>

7̶69	3⁸2	7͞5
x 3	x 6	x 4
25²	120	827

The use of the number symbols in the above answers is an excellent example of right-left directional confusion. The problems were done by an intelligent twelve-year-old boy who had a very poor rote memory. He could not remember his multiplication tables or his addition or subtraction combinations, and he managed his answers by counting—sometimes rather ingeniously. He verbalized his difficulties very well: "I get all mixed up. Where do I start?"

His reasoning and computation on the above problems were as follows:

Problem (A)   9 x 3 = 27;   put down 2 and carry 7;   6 x 3 = 18;   18 + 7 = 25.

Problem (B)   3 x 6 = 18;   put down 1 and carry 8;   2 x 6 = 12;   12 + 8 = 20.

Problem (C)   7 x 4 = 28;   put down 8 and carry 2;   5 x 4 = 25;   25 + 2 = 27!

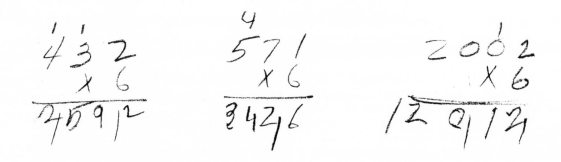

In these problems, although he managed to do his multiplication correctly, he became confused over which direction to take in marking off thousands. In the first problem, he decided to mark off from <u>both</u> sides, "so I would be sure to get it right!"

Examples of left-right directional confusions
on part of twelve-year-old sixth-grade boy.

insecurity in the concept of right and left,[20] and that impairment of "directional function disturbs principally the comprehension of symbols"—letters, numbers, music notes, and Morse code.[21]

In discussing the application of theories of Gestalt psychology (perception of an object as a whole)[22] to the reading process, he states that reading and writing problems in congenital word-blindness can be looked upon as impaired Gestalt function; however, he believes it probable that impaired Gestalt function results "because there is primarily a disturbance of directional function."[23] He explains that while direction may not be of crucial importance when one looks at an object such as a photograph, it is of major importance when one has to consider words, with their letter sequences, since the "phonetic functions of the word's letters depend on their being perceived in their right places within the word entity."[24] In specific language disability the insecurity of direction is indicated by the confusions in direction previously described on page 10, and by the types of errors made--rotations, reversals, etc.

A different sort of approach has been undertaken by Donald E. P. Smith and Patricia M. Carrigan in their search for a neuro-chemical reason for the hesitant, irregular, or distorted responses among the S.L.D.

is even begun. He is trained so that his "neurological organization" is either all right sided or all left sided. See Carl H. Delacato, The Treatment and Prevention of Reading Problems, Charles C Thomas, Springfield, Ill., 1959.

19. Samuel T. Orton, M.D., Reading, Writing, and Speech Problems in Children, W. W. Norton and Company, Inc., New York, N.Y., 1937.

Dr. Orton's work has been the inspiration for much subsequent experimental medical and teaching research in the area of language disabilities. He is held in such esteem that the Orton Society, founded in his memory, concerns itself with furthering knowledge through a continuing study of these disabilities, and with programs of correction and prevention. The Bulletin of the Orton Society, published annually, performs a needed service with its articles on research and its reports on teaching experimentation. The present address is Box 153, Pomfret, Conn.

20. Knud Hermann, M.D., Reading Disability, Charles C Thomas, Springfield, Ill., 1959, pp. 136, 137 (with permission of the original publisher, Munksgaard A/S, Copenhagen).

21. Ibid., p. 140.

22. "According to Gestalt psychology, an object is perceived in its totality, not by the successive aggregation of parts to form a whole—the constituent parts are perceived simultaneously." Ibid., pp. 142-143. An example would be a triangle of any size.

23. Ibid., p. 144.

24. Ibid., p. 145.

learners. In general, they are concerned with some chemical abnormality affecting regular and proper firing across the neural synapse. (This is the point of contact between dendrites, the branching protoplasmic parts of the nerve cell.) The authors consider, too, that "Synaptic transmission and neural activity generally appear to be influenced by endocrine functioning."[25]

This presentation of neurological research concerning cause does not pretend to be complete, but it is enough to point out the direction of neurological investigation.

Before completing this discussion on specific language disability, two clarifications should be made. What, for one, is the difference between children with this difficulty and those who are slow learners?

The distinction may be made that specific language disability children are slow because of their particular difficulty or combination of difficulties (reversals, poor visual memory for words, etc.). It will be remembered that all children with these problems do not necessarily have all the problems, "but each has enough to distinguish him from a child who is. . .a 'slow reader'" for other reasons.[26]

The other needed clarification concerns the difference between a language disability and a learning disability. This distinction is made by de Hirsch, who defines these entities carefully. She points out that language disability may manifest itself as, for example, a specific reading difficulty. It is a primary cause for not learning and can produce resultant emotional difficulties. "A secondary reading difficulty might be the result of a variety of causes: physical illness, poor teaching, frequent change of schools, environmental pathology. None of these should be confused with the primary variety of the disorder."[27] On the other hand, a learning disability is identified as coming from primary causes such as low intelligence or basic emotional disturbance.

---

25. Donald E. P. Smith and Patricia M. Carrigan, The Nature of Reading Disability, Harcourt, Brace & World, Inc., New York, N.Y., 1959, p. 90.
26. J. Roswell Gallagher, M.D., "Can't Spell, Can't Read," Atlantic Monthly, Vol. 181, No. 6, June, 1948, p. 36.
27. Katrina de Hirsch, L.C.S.T., "Specific Dyslexia or Strephosymbolia," Folia Phoniatrica, Vol. 4, No. 4 (1952), p. 233 (published by S. Karger, Basel/New York).

For a diagnostic breakdown of language difficulties,[28] the substance of the previous paragraph is organized into the following outline:

A. Nonspecific language disability

1. Poor intellectual endowment

2. Basic emotional disturbance

These conditions constitute a <u>learning</u> <u>disability</u>. In such cases, probably all schoolwork suffers; reading, spelling, and writing problems are <u>nonspecific</u> and secondary to the learning disability.

B. Specific language disability

This condition constitutes a <u>language</u> <u>disability</u>. In this case, reading, spelling, and writing problems are <u>specific</u>. The child with this disability <u>can</u> learn, but learning through reading, or sometimes by writing, is disproportionately difficult for him. He is the one who may say he could learn if someone would read to him; or if someone would listen to him "say back" his lesson, rather than require him to write it down. It is easily understood that his language problems give rise to emotional problems which are secondary to the primary problem of S.L.D.

C. Other causes for language difficulties include:

1. Frequent absence

2. Frequent change of schools

3. Poor teaching

4. Speech disorders

5. Physical illness, and eye and ear defects

6. Brain damage

7. Factors in the environment

Of course, children who have problems in both specific and nonspecific categories are not unheard-of. Even with these children it is helpful to recognize and treat a specific language disability as well as, for example, a basic emotional difficulty.

And now, a concluding question--what about life in the classroom for children who are scholastically disabled by specific language disability?

Some indication of what the individual with this difficulty has to

---

28. <u>Ibid.</u>, pp. 232-234.

endure in school is given by Anna Gillingham, who has had long association with these children and their concerns. Her comment on their predicament is as follows:

> Often more able than the majority of his class to understand
> content, he feels himself regarded as stupid; trying much harder
> than the boy in the next seat, he finds himself reprimanded for care-
> lessness and indolence. He is as bewildered when expected to get
> ideas from the printed page or to express his own ideas in writing
> as he would be if told that if only he "tried hard" enough he could
> wiggle his ears. He just doesn't know how to try, and the outstand-
> ing lesson he has learned in school is that effort will result in fail-
> ure, an appalling lesson.[29]

In my own experience I have become well acquainted with this situation, too. One year, while teaching a group of girls of mixed ages I wit-
nessed the misery of a sixth-grade girl with specific language disability.
(Her score on the Revised Stanford-Binet Scale, Form M, was 108.) Sensitivity concerning her reading and spelling inadequacies and her stumbling
performance helped to set her apart from the others. Some of the girls
were seventh- and eighth-graders, and they were at times unmercifully
cruel in their attitude of boredom and their impatience with her. The
following is an excerpt from a letter which she wrote, with some spelling
help, to a friend:

> I'm associating wich (with) the other girls now. They seem to like
> me now. Boy am I glad too. At the end of the week they will tell
> me if I can be in the club. I hope I can though. Do you?

It takes little imagination to realize the build-up of mounting psychological damage in such individuals--the frustration, the discouragement,
the feelings of inferiority.

It takes little imagination, too, to realize what complexities these
children present for conscientious teachers and administrators. How easy
it would be to assume that these learning difficulties were basically an
expression of an emotional problem.

And what about the parents? Their anxieties over these matters are

29. Anna Gillingham, "The Language Function," in The Independent School
Bulletin, the Independent Schools Education Board, Milton, Mass., Jan., 1951.

acute. Even to some of the most stable of families it has been implied that a deep emotional malady, due to some family problem, has been the prime cause. They wonder how or where they have been guilty.

Report on Teaching Techniques for
Specific Language Disability

In this country two time-tested remedial approaches have been developed to help those individuals with specific language disability. One approach was developed by Grace Fernald who classified reading disability cases in two groups, (1) those of "total or extreme disability," and (2) those of "partial disability."[30] The center for her work has been at the Clinic School at the University of California at Los Angeles.

The other approach was developed by Anna Gillingham and her associate Bessie W. Stillman.[31] Miss Gillingham worked in conjunction with the neurologist, Samuel T. Orton, who, at the New York Neurological Institute, did extensive research on reading, writing, and speech problems in specific language disability children. As research associate, Anna Gillingham formulated remedial techniques, based on Dr. Orton's research, to train the children in this category. She is known, too, for her early-identification testing program and for her training program for teachers.

The methods of both Fernald and Gillingham, when properly employed, have an excellent record of success. Fernald considered her method as an "application of established psychological principles,"[32] whereas Gillingham's method may be thought of as a neurophysiological approach. Actually, both methods have in view the same end--building association for words by linking auditory, visual, and kinesthetic avenues; but the procedures for achieving this goal differ.

---

30. From _Remedial Techniques in Basic School Subjects_, by Grace M. Fernald. Copyright, 1943. McGraw-Hill Book Co., New York, N.Y. Used by permission. (Chaps. V - VI).

31. Anna Gillingham and Bessie W. Stillman, _Remedial Training for Children with Specific Disability in Reading, Spelling and Penmanship_. Distributed by Anna Gillingham, 25 Parkview Avenue, Bronxville 8, N.Y. Fifth edition, 1956, and sixth edition 1960.

32. _Op. cit._, p. v.

The methods developed by Borel-Maisonny in France and by Norrie in Denmark should also be mentioned, not only because they have been time-tested and successful, but also because they point up the fact that specific language disability (called word blindness in Denmark and dyslexia in France) is world-wide and not a product of the United States or its educational methods. These outstanding teachers also have used methods designed to reinforce the memory of language symbols and are people who have been associated with neurologists in Denmark (Dr. Hermann and Dr. Skydsgaard) and in France (Dr. Zazzo, Dr. Ajuriaguerra, and their colleagues).[33]

Since attention in this chapter is directed to the findings of the medical profession and those associated with it in the area of specific language disability, the teaching techniques under discussion are those based on neurological findings.

In considering these techniques it is helpful to group the children in terms of these age levels: kindergarten-primary, intermediate, and junior-senior high school.

Kindergarten-Primary

Obviously, the early identification of children with potentiality for specific language disability is a needed answer and the practical answer.

Significant work at early age levels is being accomplished in various ways—in certain language clinics and in a few schools, both private and public. For instance, most careful attention to experimentation (with results which have implications for schools) is being carried on under the direction of Katrina de Hirsch at the Pediatric Language Disorder Clinic, Vanderbilt Clinic, Columbia-Presbyterian Medical Center, New York City. A child is referred to this clinic through pediatric psychiatry. He is given tests which are appropriate in determining whether or not he may

33. S. Borel-Maisonny, in L'Apprentissage de la Lecture et Ses Troubles —Les Dyslexies D'Evolution, Presses Universitaires de France, Paris, 1952, pp. 400-444.

Edith Norrie, Ordblinde Undervisning med fonetisk saellekasse, Nyt Nordisk Forlag Arnold Busck, Copenhagen, 1960.

have future reading disability, but also are "meant to indicate the areas in which a child's performance lags." In de Hirsch's opinion, the tests should supply, too, the information to give direction for particular techniques to be used in future training.

To date the conclusions here from testing and experimentation indicate that children with potential language disabilities have trouble in the areas of motor, perceptual, and emotional integration. Says Mrs. de Hirsch:

"Not all children suffering from potential reading difficulties are primarily emotionally disturbed. However, their basic developmental lag in physiological-psychological functioning makes them especially susceptible to adverse educational experiences and as a result they often develop secondary emotional difficulties very early."[34]

At the Francis W. Parker School, an old established private school in Chicago, a seven-year experiment in testing, identifying, and teaching specific language disability children by Gillingham methods has been completed.[35]

Placed in small special groups of five to seven were those children whose family histories showed a tendency for specific language disability, whose Binets, motor data, and visual, auditory, and kinesthetic recall gave evidence that they would not succeed with usual first-grade reading procedures. The special groups were taught by carefully planned alphabetic word-building methods. (This system will be defined briefly later.)

The success of the experiment, now over ten years old and supported by Metropolitan Achievement Test scores, is noteworthy--96 per cent. At present, according to The Development Council Bulletin, the Parker School has plans for establishing a Gillingham Reading Center where teachers can

34. Katrina de Hirsch, "Tests Designed to Discover Potential Reading Difficulties at the Six-Year-Old Level," The American Journal of Orthopsychiatry, Vol. XXVII, No. 3, July, 1957, pp. 575, 576.

35. The First Seven Years of the Gillingham Reading Program at Francis W. Parker School, as presented at the Gillingham Institute, Jan. 26, 1957. Francis W. Parker School, 330 Webster Ave., Chicago 14, Ill.

be properly trained and where research can be carried out.[36] Brief
accounts of this experiment have appeared in two popular magazines.[37] [38]

In another private school, which may or may not recognize specific
language disability by that name, it was observed that certain children who
could not read at the chronological age of six years had one or more of
the following problems:

(1) Speech delay [did not "hear" sounds well]

(2) Poor directional sense

(3) Agraphia [or Dysgraphia--didn't use the hand well for writing]

(4) Poor perceptions [likenesses and differences not clearly defined]

Consequently, there was put into effect a program of educating the
parents not to expect all children to read at six years. Further, as a
training measure, phonetics through games was put in operation for five-
year-olds in the second half of the kindergarten year. In the first grade,
emphasis on phonics was continued and writing was begun early.[39]

Moreover, the matter of using specially prepared training material
for prevention of failures has been explored at the kindergarten level.
In a further effort to avert failures, Anna Gillingham in association with
Beth H. Slingerland devised exercises and games, all carefully designed
to develop abilities necessary for reading success. "We asked ourselves,
How can we foster the growth of some of these prerequisite abilities?"[40]

The exercises and games containing the preparatory training are
printed on individual cards and are grouped in five classifications. The
classifications are each printed on differently colored cards which contain
the following:

36. The Development Council Bulletin, Francis W. Parker School, Dec.
1959, p. 2.

37. Darlene Geis, "The School Where Johnny Does Read," Coronet, Vol. 40,
No. 6, Oct., 1956, pp. 86-90.

38. "Learning to Read," Newsweek, Vol. IV, No. 15, Oct. 12, 1959, p. 110.

39. Notes from the comments of Dr. Cecilia Brinton, symposium on "Is
There a Best Way to Teach Reading?" in Palo Alto, Calif., Mar. 26, 1958.

40. Beth H. Slingerland and Anna Gillingham, Training in Prerequisites for
Beginning Reading, p. 3. Published by the authors, 25 Parkview Ave., Bronxville,
N.Y. The exercises and games have been obtainable through the authors.

Speech Practice—provides opportunity through speech and action for such skills as matching, classifying, and categorizing objects or pictures, for differentiation of categories, for language usage, for experience in observation and deduction, and for reproducing stories.

Orientation Games—give training in right and left direction, before and after progression, vertical position, et cetera.

Visual Recall
Auditory Recall } —provide exercises and games to develop and
Kinesthetic Recall } strengthen recall in these areas.

It is encouraging to know that pioneering in recognition of specific language disability and in training is not limited to medical facilities and private schools. At Peterborough, New Hampshire, and Lincoln, Massachusetts, Robert L. Filbin,[41] aided by Dr. Richard Eustis, has had the ingenuity to recognize and tackle the problem of specific language disability in the public schools, to orient and train teachers, and to organize programs which make it possible to teach these children in the regular classroom with their classmates.

In collaboration with his teachers[42] at Peterborough Filbin has compiled two brief mimeographed manuals entitled Identifying and Screening Children at the First Grade Level Who May Have Difficulty in the Language Arts [43] and The Alphabetic Phonetic Method—A Technique for Teaching Children With Specific Language Disability in the Classroom. It is my understanding that the substance of these manuals, along with a report of results achieved, will be available through publication.

---

41. Robert L. Filbin, Supervising Principal, Lincoln, Mass.
42. Barbara Carll, Myrtie Kullgren, Dorothy Morris.
43. This manual alerts the teachers to the characteristics of specific language disability through a check list (which they use), and it describes a few simple tests. These tests are given to check (1) auditory perception for listening, echo speech, memory, discrimination, rhyming, and initial sounds; (2) evidence of mixed dominance (directional sense may be determined by the examiner, who draws a simple arrow →, and distracts the child's attention for a few moments, after which the child draws the arrow from recall; this performance is repeated about twenty times; many of the child's arrows may be reproduced in reverse—which is considered significant in anticipating a problem not only with direction but with recall); (3) handedness and ambidexterity; (4) sense of rhythm; and (5) footedness.

At Peterborough[44] and Lincoln groups of children who could not be expected to learn by usual reading procedures are not taught by what Gillingham refers to as "analytical" or "functional" phonics (i.e., breaking down known sight-words into phonetic parts). Rather, they are taught by another phonic approach, Gillingham's alphabetic word-building method, which she speaks of as the Alphabetic Approach--one rooted in the history of language itself and based upon the "concept of combining letters to form words. . ."[45]

Since it is not fair to attempt to describe in a few words such a carefully thought-out method, the following explanation is intended merely to give an idea of the initial approach. In the beginning the children are taught a few consonants whose sounds and forms cannot be confused, and several short vowel sounds. As soon as these are mastered by name and sound, three-letter words are put together. The addition of new letters and combinations follows, producing new words that are gradually built into sentences and stories. Proper sound blending is all important, and a paramount need is that the lessons be structured. For purposes of association, the sounds have <u>key</u> <u>words</u> to help the learner, (e.g., ă as in <u>apple</u>, ĕ as <u>elephant</u>, etc.). Equipment involves packets of phonics drill cards, phonetic words, materials to convey syllable concepts, phonetic reading material, and later on, <u>Webster's Elementary Dictionary</u>.[46]

This alphabetic system is highly organized and involves reasoning to build step-by-step mastery of the language. Association for letters, sounds, syllables, and words is developed through sequential language experience which forges links among auditory, visual, and kinesthetic pathways. The basic guide for this approach is the Gillingham and Stillman

44. Robert L. Filbin, "Prescription for the Johnny Who Can't Read," <u>Elementary English</u>, Vol. 34, Dec., 1957, pp. 559-561.

45. Letter from Anna Gillingham to Editor of <u>Elementary English</u>, Vol. 35, No. 2, Feb., 1958, p. 121. Reprinted with the permission of the National Council of Teachers of English and Anna Gillingham.

46. <u>Webster's Elementary Dictionary</u>, 1956, and <u>Webster's New Secondary School Dictionary</u>, G. & C. Merriam Co., Springfield, Mass., 1959.

Manual.[47] A proper adaptation of it must be made for the first and second grades.

With reference again to the Peterborough project, Mr. Filbin reported the system as being used with success and the results at the end of the second year as "astonishing." The children are grouped together, but are not considered a problem group; they remain with their regular class. The plan is to continue the work with this group from the second through the fifth grade.[48]

A visit to Lincoln was an absorbing experience. A second grade was observed in action. The class was divided into four reading groups. The specific language disability reading section of about five children was being drilled by Gillingham's Alphabetic Approach techniques. They went through their drill with tremendous enthusiasm and sustained interest. From one of the other groups, four children for whom this type of instruction was helpful, too, joined the specific language disability section for a part of the practice. The remainder of the class was busy with the various activities listed on the blackboard.

The teacher was delighted with the progress the specific language disability children were making. She was inventive, resourceful, and imaginative with the drill. She was an excellent classroom manager, and it was evident that she enjoyed the challenge of applying such diverse methods in her classroom.

At nearby Wayland a similar program of screening, teacher orientation, and adaptation of Gillingham methods for primary and intermediate children is in progress. The interesting fact is that enlightened school administrators in the Wayland public school system have taken the initiative and have enlisted the aid of The Adolescent Unit at the Children's Hospital Medical Center, Boston, As a result. Mrs. Reta V. Buchan, the experienced and devoted director of The Adolescent Unit's Language

47. Anna Gillingham and Bessie W. Stillman, Remedial Training for Children With Specific Disability in Reading, Spelling and Penmanship. Distributed by Anna Gillingham, 25 Parkview Ave., Bronxville 8, N.Y., Sixth edition, 1960.
48. Robert L. Filbin, "Prescription for the Johnny Who Can't Read," Elementary English, Vol. 34, Dec., 1957, pp. 559-561.

Training Clinic, aided by other trained personnel, has assisted this school system. Teacher training as well as teaching and testing services--when needed--are supplied.

It is to be emphasized that the educational leaders and classroom teachers engaged in these programs of adaptation are grounded in the principles underlying the Gillingham method and experienced in employing it. Liaison with their programs is maintained by doctors and psychologists who have knowledge and understanding of specific language disability. This kind of cooperation among trained and experienced persons in three professions not only serves the children well, but also protects the method from misapplication.

Comment on Upper Levels

In moving ahead, we will consider the children in this category of specific language disability who are of intermediate and high school age levels--learners who could be described as among those being "plowed under."[49] They have been laboring for some time with this situation in varying degrees of academic and psychological distress.

For children of these age levels who need help, again the Manual by Gillingham and Stillman is most comprehensive.[50] Ostensibly, it is designed for remedial, tutorial purposes; but there is a monumental amount of valuable, assembled material with possibilities for group adaptation.

The Manual explains the problem and provides careful steps in training. It is emphasized that the purpose is "not to teach phonics but to show how correct phonics can be applied to the needs of such children. . ."[51]

Intermediate

At this age level, and older, it is believed that the "spelling errors

---

49. It "would have to be demonstrated that quality need not be plowed under by quantity." Fred M. Hechinger, "Wanted: Quality as Well as Quantity," The Saturday Review, Vol. XXXIX, No. 36, Sept. 8, 1956, pp. 19-20, 55.

50. Anna Gillingham and Bessie W. Stillman, Remedial Training for Children with Specific Disability in Reading, Spelling and Penmanship. Distributed by Anna Gillingham, 25 Parkview Avenue, Bronxville 8, N.Y. Sixth edition, 1960. (In the 1960 edition chap. iv is for upper-grade and high school pupils.)

51. Ibid., Part Two, Remedial Procedures. Fourth edition, 1946, p. 2.

made by children who have a specific language disability are the best single diagnostic criteria. . ."[52]

A glance at the following spelling test written by a sixth-grade boy reveals some characteristic troubles: reversals, confusions, inaccuracy in distinguishing vowel sounds, probably poor visual memory for what the word looked like, and lack of any strong association for relating sight and sound.

(Grade 6, age 12)

52. J. Roswell Gallagher, M.D., "Specific Language Disability: A Cause of Scholastic Failure," New England Journal of Medicine, Vol. 242, No. 12, Mar. 23, 1950, p. 438.

If this boy were receiving medical care and advice from a doctor who recognized specific language disability as a cause of school failure, his language difficulties would be assessed in relation to any other problems, physical or emotional, which he might have. Ambidexterity, family history, etc., would be checked also, and his language difficulties would be tested. The latter need not be an involved process. The boy should read orally a short but demanding paragraph, write a list of spelling words from dictation, and write a short description of a picture. Such a picture "may have some useful psychologic content and will furnish an opportunity to note the manner and quality of the handwriting."[53] These simple language-testing practices could be useful in assisting teachers interested in identifying specific language disability.

In the public school systems already mentioned where this condition is recognized, the intermediate-level children with the handicap receive instruction in Gillingham techniques, or adaptations of them.[54]

Allied with the Gillingham approach are the materials developed by Mrs. Mildred Plunkett, of the Massachusetts General Hospital Language Clinic. These include spelling workbooks for both elementary and secondary levels,[55] [56] and a manual and exercises for the left-handed.[57] [58] It is obvious that these materials have been developed by a teacher whose first-hand experience with specific language disability is complete.

53. Ibid., p. 439.

54. In one group observed, six intermediate-level boys with rather severe S.L.D. problems were in a separate room working as a group with an experienced trainee from The Adolescent Unit's Language Training Clinic. These boys kept notebooks and were engaged in building their associations for a particular phonetic principle ("ou," "ow," etc.) through sight, sound, articulation, and writing.

55. Mildred B. Plunkett, A Spelling Workbook for Corrective Drill for Elementary Grades, Robert G. Hall, Manter Hall School, 71 Mount Auburn Street, Cambridge 38, Mass., 1956.
    (1960 publications at the elementary level by Mildred Plunkett and Carol Z. Peck are entitled A Spelling Workbook for Early Primary Corrective Work, Books I and II, Educators Publishing Service, Cambridge, Mass.

56. Mildred B. Plunkett, A Spelling Workbook Emphasizing Rules and Generalizations for Corrective Drill, Robert G. Hall, Manter Hall School, 71 Mount Auburn Street, Cambridge 38, Mass., 1949.

57. Mildred B. Plunkett, A Writing Manual for Teaching the Left-Handed, Manter Hall School, 71 Mount Auburn Street, Cambridge, Mass., 1954.

58. Mildred B. Plunkett, Writing Exercises for the Left-Handed, Manter Hall School, 71 Mount Auburn Street, Cambridge, Mass., 1954.

It is obvious, too, that the spelling workbooks represent constructive, organized help for any language arts program. The lessons require the student to apply what he has learned, and they provide the teacher with a plan for integrating auditory, visual, and kinesthetic pathways.

Related to the Gillingham approach, also, is a spelling curriculum for classroom use written by Sally B. Childs, of New York.[59] The words for study are from an Arthur I. Gates list and the spelling range is from grades two to eight. The author explains the division of the words into three groups: (1) those words for which the child is "held responsible for spelling without study" because they (a) are phonetic, or (b) have already been learned, or (c) have rules or generalizations already learned (Group A); (2) those words which will become part of Group A as the necessary rule or generalization is mastered (Group B); and (3) those words which must be learned for themselves, since no rule or generalization previously learned applies (Group C). The method can be applied to any list of words needing to be learned and, with altered criteria, even to foreign languages.

This spelling curriculum is scientifically constructed; it furnishes a workable plan for applying the neurophysiological approach to spelling; it has an excellent reputation, and is now in use in nearly a hundred schools and reading centers. In one public school system observed, it was in use in all regular classes.

Junior-Senior High School

Turning to a consideration of the junior-senior high school, let us think a moment about the classroom teacher. How can he reach these individuals? He has a particularly challenging task in helping them. These young people may be too embarrassed, too sensitive, too discouraged to apply the techniques that would help them. They may resist special attention in the presence of their classmates. They underrate their intelligence. They may have developed a "What's-the-use?" attitude.

59. Sally B. Childs, A Spelling Curriculum, Sally B. Childs, 9 Old Westbrook Road, Clinton, Conn. Third printing, 1956.

29

They are weighed down by inarticulate frustrations. What can we do now to retrieve these able minds?

There is much to be done. Teachers and administrators should be encouraged to identify these young people, and to persist in searching for success in grouping them and helping them in the ways they can accept with some feelings of self-respect. This last is the crux so far as the students are concerned.

After identification and grouping, the classes should function more successfully if certain conditions were carried out. These conditions suggest the following:

1. Diagnosing individual difficulties by testing oral reading, spelling, and written work. For example, poor auditory memory for individual sounds and component parts of words may be the cause of poor spelling. Be sure the individual understands his problem, or problems, and plan treatment with him.

2. Presenting to the pupils concerned a careful explanation of the "three-fold language pattern," which is the ability to recognize, to sound out, and to write the word.[60] (This explanation may be accompanied by explanatory charts which diagram the inferred working of the sensory and motor avenues of learning—the visual, auditory, and kinesthetic avenues. The role of association should be explained, also. It is important for young people to understand that the sensory motor avenues, linked by association, all need to work together in order to establish satisfactory language function.)

3. Attempting to manage within the group a two-part program— an individual program and a group program. (Each pupil should work on the individual tasks which meet his own particular problem; and he should work, also, with the group as a whole on lessons and material suitable for all. Drama and other literature offer many resources for group attention.)

4. Creating self-confidence in each individual by showing and

---

60. Anna Gillingham, "The Language Function," in The Independent School Bulletin, the Independent Schools Education Board, Milton, Mass., Jan., 1951.

explaining to him a profile of his <u>strengths</u>. (Since these students commonly describe themselves as "dumb," this revelation is a <u>must</u>.)

5. Finding an increased number of teachers who have sensitivity for the students' predicament, who are willing to build their own basic background of knowledge about these difficulties, and who are able to put the teaching techniques into practice.

6. Maintaining wholehearted administrative support.

7. Investigating practices that have been used elsewhere.

8. Investigating materials that have been compiled and used successfully by experienced specific language disability teachers.

9. Scheduling time for explanations of the problem and the program to parents.

10. Polling the students for their thinking on possible approaches. One thoughtful boy volunteered:

  a. The term Remedial English, as a name for these courses, is very damaging to the students' morale. "Your friends ask you what you are taking. You don't like to tell them 'Remedial.' A much more appealing or catchy name should be thought out. Maybe, just English."

  b. Short daily tests, of the five-to-ten-minute variety (not "exams"), on spelling, application of grammar usage, etc., had been helpful to him.

  c. The counselors might be helpful in persuading students "to take something like that."

Another boy suggested:

  a. Permitting each student to read in his own area of interest— fossils, stars, space, etc.

  b. Exercising of choice to stay with or drop the course should be allowed; that is, open the course at the beginning of the school year so that the student can give it a week's trial.

  c. "Getting the right teacher" is a must—one who is a "sort of buddy with the boys," interested in their interests, and having a wide general knowledge of what boys like—sports, "hot rods," music, art. "This is the kind of teacher that makes the difference."

Reports on Applications for Whole Classes

In termininating these reports and observations on teaching techniques for specific language disability, the final accounts of interest are a magazine article and a book that report applications for whole classes.

Evidently, expanded application of the Alphabetic Approach for entire classrooms is now in use. (See p. 24.) Gillingham reports that (1) Mary Davidson, formerly head of the primary department of Fieldston Lower School, New York City, is "now using the Alphabetic Approach with whole classes in the Oakwood School in North Hollywood, California"; and that (2) Mabel Bennett, of St. Paul's School, Baltimore, Maryland, used this approach with a first grade of sixteen pupils beginning in the fall of 1956.[61] She quotes test scores for the group in June, 1957 (Metropolitan Achievement Tests - Primary I Battery: Form R), as follows:

Median ..... Gr. 3.2
Highest..... Gr. 4.3   } Independent School Norms
Lowest ..... Gr. 2.0 (two children)

Gillingham states that her experience has gradually brought her to the conclusion that there is no clear differentiation "between the potential reading failure and the child who learns with a slight degree of success. . . .With the almost universal uproar about poor spelling, we can afford to give some training to the kinesthetic and auditory aspects of the language pattern at the beginning."[62]

The additional point of importance is the fact that a child may learn to read with facility, but run into spelling difficulties later on. In other words, "Recognition is apparently easier than recall."[63] Thus, he may recognize the whole word, but be unable to manage the parts in written exposition.

The other program for teaching the entire class is known as the Unified Phonics Method, devised by Romalda and Walter Spalding. The

61. Letter from Anna Gillingham to Editor, Elementary English, Vol. 35, No. 2, Feb., 1958, pp. 121-122.

62. Ibid., p. 121. Reprinted with the permission of the National Council of Teachers of English and Anna Gillingham.

63. Quoted, with the permission of the publisher, from Norman L. Munn, "Learning in Children," in Leonard Carmichael (editor), Manual of Child Psychology, second edition, John Wiley and Sons, Inc., New York, N.Y., 1954, p. 414.

results for both reading and spelling are reported in their book, The Writing Road to Reading.[64] The children learn to write the sound combinations before they are exposed to them in the reading process. Years ago, writing before reading was established as a highly successful technique by Montessori, too, and there would seem to be developmental basis for this practice. The Unified Phonics Method has had several years of successful application in the primary grades of Hawaii's parochial school system.

Important Things to Know
About These Teaching Techniques

What is vital to teaching children with specific language disability is training that establishes and strengthens associations. "To this end all nervous pathways are mobilized in order to help link the visual to the auditory structure of the word and relate both to meaning."[65]

"We need to analyze carefully where the trouble lies . . . so as to provide him [the child] with the links he has failed to establish; we must utilize the discriminations he is able to make, and employ all sensory channels available so as to reinforce necessary associations."[66]

All children cannot learn to read by the whole word or sight method. Unqualified acceptance of this fact underlies the Gillingham technique. For instance, in the area of visual recall there are those whose vision is excellent, but whose visual recall (memory) for words may be either poor, or uncertain, or non-functioning. Such children are unable to remember words by recognizing or recalling what they look like.[67]

---

64. Romalda Bishop Spalding, with Walter T. Spalding, The Writing Road to Reading, Whiteside, Inc., and William Morrow and Company, New York, N.Y., 1957.

65. Katrina de Hirsch, "Specific Dyslexia or Strephosymbolia," Folia Phoniatrica, Vol. 4, No. 4 (1952), p. 246 (published by S. Karger, Basel/New York).

66. Ibid., pp. 239-240.

67. "Certainly, if reading is to be very generally learned and if purely visual methods are to be employed for the average child, facilities must be set up to differentiate between those children who can be expected to learn by purely visual methods and those who, for neurologic reasons, are incapable of this type of learning. Failure to recognize this fundamental fact has caused untold grief to

(continued on next page)

Trying to learn to recognize 150 to 200 sight words opens the door to failure; so trying to learn by looking is for them disastrous, indeed. In fact, when describing his own experience, Warren, (previously presented), said: "Watching Mom write used to look like a bunch of bumps to me—tall bumps and short bumps." This boy had no real mental concept of individual letters or combinations of letters, or of words, and no association on which to pin them. In the early stages of reading, too, perhaps he could not distinguish foreground (printing) from background (the page).

Similarly, in the area of auditory recall, even though a child has perfect hearing, he may have poor auditory recall (memory) for words. He may not be able to think of a particular word, although he has heard it spoken many times; or he may exhibit uncertainty or confusion in pronouncing it. One young woman, thinking back on her school struggles, told me: "If I couldn't remember what the word sounded like and how it was spoken, I couldn't remember what it was used for or how it was written."

And for those persistent cases of auditory uncertainty and confusion in pronouncing words a few examples may be helpful. For instance, to one boy a story character, Lem, was always "Lim." Distinguishing the vowels "e" and "i" through the auditory pathway is very difficult for some children. Other less common types of auditory confusions are those which reveal a mixed-up type of pronounciation, such as "driffin" for "different," or those in which whole syllables are omitted in speech, such as "totalarian" for totalitarian. Furthermore, although there may be excellent recall for repeating entire sentences or isolated words, the individual sounds in words may mean nothing when the student tries to spell. That is, when attempting to spell orally or to write a word from dictation, there may be little or no spelling tie-up with the spoken

many children, untold worry to many parents and teachers, and, of course, a great deal of expense to the taxpayer." Edwin M. Cole, M.D., "Specific Reading Disability: A Problem in Integration and Adaptation," American Journal of Opthalmology, Vol. 34, No. 2, Feb., 1951, p. 231.

sounds ("effcet" instead of "effect," for instance). In short, the tie-up between auditory and kinesthetic pathways for the whole word and its parts has not become sufficiently integrated for adequate oral spelling or written-language use.

In the category of kinesthetic difficulties, there are children who find it hard to learn to write (dysgraphia). Such a problem may exist along with reading and spelling difficulties, or it may exist by itself. According to Orton, a child in this situation may have legible handwriting yet be unable to write with enough speed for ordinary purposes; or he may demonstrate poor or illegible handwriting. Often, there may be a history of a change from left- to right-handedness in infancy or enforcement of the use of the right hand in writing. If the child is a natural left-hander, he may need reorientation.[68] (For instance, if he is a mirror writer, he probably can be helped by the Fernald technique of starting at the left margin of the paper or blackboard to trace his words. There is no way to go but to the right!) Other evidence of writing difficulty may show in those who have not established handedness.[69] [70]

Hermann, too, makes an intensely interesting and careful appraisal of writing difficulties in congenital word-blindness. He classifies as ideational dysgraphia the inability to remember how to make the shape of the letter, and as motor dysgraphia the inability to produce the proper writing motions, although the shape of the letter is remembered. For the individual having a combination of both problems, he terms the condition ideomotor dysgraphia.[71] Anyone who has ever tried to teach a child with any dysgraphia will be absorbed by this account.

68. Samuel Torrey Orton, M.D., Reading, Writing and Speech Problems in Children, W. W. Norton and Company, Inc., New York, N.Y., 1937, pp. 99-105.
69. Ibid., pp. 99-110. A comprehensive description of writing difficulties is given by Orton.
70. For information on left-handedness a mimeographed publication, "The Sinister Hand," was issued by the University of California ("Public Information - Radio," Broadcast #3457-U.E. 1444x, Feb. 5, 1956).
71. Knud Hermann, M.D., Reading Disability, Charles C Thomas, Springfield, Ill., 1959, pp. 49-74.

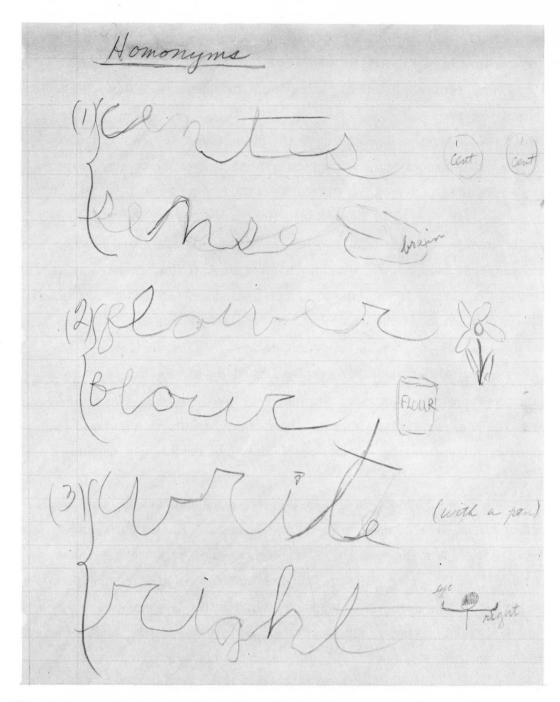

This is the handwriting of an intelligent ten-year-old boy who had a difficult time learning how to write, and who had not achieved adequate usage.　(Grade 5.)

The next consideration is help for the child in understanding the nature of his specific language disability problem.　Already has been mentioned the boost to morale given by pointing out the assets—native ability, skills, and aptitudes as indicated by tests and other performances.

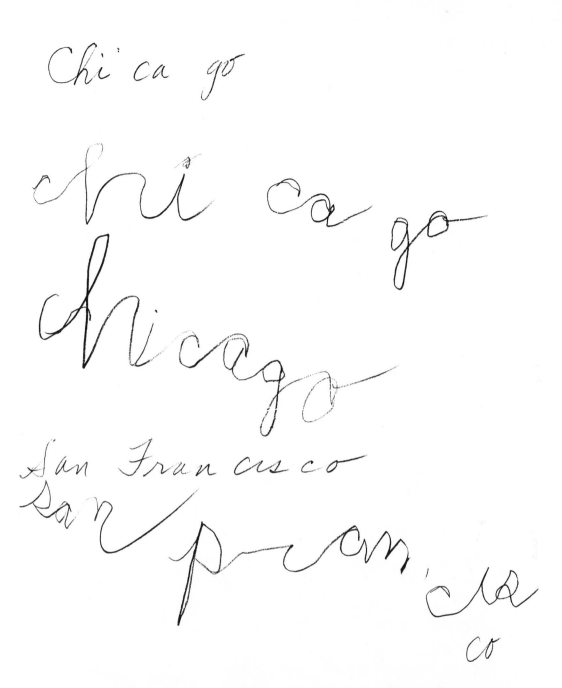

For this pupil, both the recollection of how to make the letters and the motor act of writing them were difficult. The shape of the letters had to be taught by association; for example, the letter "r" was an "old tree stump." (Fifth-grade boy, age 10.)

Already, too, have been mentioned the advantages of the child's thoroughly understanding that his difficulty lies not in deficient ability to learn, but in the special way he needs to learn.

In addition, some notion of the growth of written language is of inestimable value. Gillingham in making her explanation to children traces by story and picture the history of how written words evolved, and how in alphabetic languages words can be likened to ideograms, (pictures representing words), for those who cannot remember the look of the word. Because words are the forms these children have difficulty remembering, they are assured they will be shown another way

Example of specific language disability in spelling and handwriting in a twelve-year-old sixth-grade boy whose score on the Verbal Scale on the Wechsler fell in the range of average ability. He was an avid reader. Obviously, spelling and handwriting problems do not necessarily denote meagerness of expression.

of remembering them—the alphabetic approach. They are told that other children like themselves have been taught successfully this way.[72]

And now help for the teacher. In spite of being repetitious here and there, it seems well to report Gillingham's emphasis on what she calls linkages. The building of the "three-fold language pattern"[73] is stressed through "the constant use of association of all of the following,—how a letter or word looks, how it sounds and how the speech organs or the hand in writing feels when producing it."[74]

Although processes of recognition, association, and use may seem natural to us, they are not easy for children with these difficulties. Their recognition, association, and use of letters, sounds, and words have to be built by careful, sequential presentation. The processes by which letters or letter combinations (phonograms) are taught are known as linkages; and although eight linkages are given, three are stressed in particular.[75] These are:

(a) The linkage which translates a "seen symbol into sound" (oral reading)[76]

V - A (Visual-Auditory)
e.g., The pupil recognizes the symbol "f" on the drill card and is able to give the sound.

(b) The linkage which translates "sound into named symbol" (oral spelling)[77]

A - A (Auditory-Auditory)
and
A - K (Auditory-Kinesthetic)
e.g., The pupil gives the name of the letter after the teacher makes the sound.

---

72. Anna Gillingham and Bessie W. Stillman, Remedial Training for Children with Specific Disability in Reading, Spelling and Penmanship. Fifth edition, 1956, pp. 25-37.
73. Anna Gillingham, "The Language Function," in The Independent School Bulletin, the Independent Schools Education Board, Milton, Mass., Jan., 1951.
74. Anna Gillingham and Bessie W. Stillman, Remedial Training for Children with Specific Disability in Reading, Spelling and Penmanship. Fifth edition, 1956, p. 17.
75. Ibid., pp. 40-42. (In the sixth edition linkages are called "phonetic associations," pp. 40-41.)
76. Ibid., p. 42.
77. Ibid.

(Added associative learning is achieved by having the pupil—
with eyes closed--give the sound of the symbol as the teacher
guides his hand in writing it.)

(c) The linkage which translates "sound into written symbol" (written
spelling)[78]

A - V (Auditory-Visual)
   and
A - K (Auditory-Kinesthetic)
   e.g., The pupil writes the symbol after the teacher makes
      the sound. He names the letters as he writes them.

Although the idea to be established is that words are built out of
phonetic units, it is to be re-emphasized that any system of phonics
will not do. It is important to repeat that the application of a correct
use of phonics to the needs of these children is what is so necessary to
their success. This point is considered so vital that I quote directly
from the Manual:

Phonics Teaching

In the present widespread controversy as to whether or not to
teach phonics, little is said about what kind of phonics to teach, or
what purpose phonics might serve. A large part of what is called
phonics teaching lays itself open to the charge of being "the grunt
and groan method," and is rightly regarded as useless if not dan-
gerous. A child who has produced the series of explosive utter-
ances (fŭh) (ĭ) (gŭh) is not likely to be helped thereby to recognize that he has pronounced the word fig. The only way that
giving the sounds of the letters in succession can suggest a word,
is to produce them so lightly and briefly that the series sounds
like the word spoken slowly.

Occasionally we are told of some child whose reading has been
spoiled by his "knowing too much phonics." Rather than being a
condemnation of phonics this is in reality a condemnation of the
way in which the sounds were taught. Not infrequently it requires
long and skillful teaching to eradicate the (ŭ) following a consonant
with its distortion of the accuracy of the consonant sound.[79]

The task of the teacher is to understand how to help the children
build the linkages and how to present the sounds.

The final aspect of teaching techniques to be pointed out is the fa-
vored use of cursive penmanship over manuscript. The experience of

---

78. Ibid.
79. Ibid., p. 39.

40

the authors of the Gillingham Manual, and mine, too, is that cursive writing is much to be preferred for pupils of this type.[80]   One reason for this is that letters in cursive (handwriting) form are not reversible, as are b and d, p and q in manuscript (printing).   Another reason is that kinesthetic learning is a strong link in establishing the memory for a letter or a word; thus the impression should be gained correctly, uncluttered by possibilities of "rotation."   Furthermore, movement in manuscript is broken, while movement in cursive is unbroken.   Here, again, it seems that kinesthetic impression is more meaningful and coherent if the motion can be a continuous flow.

Too, there is the matter of motion itself.   Children love motion, and when using cursive writing they can perform with freedom.

Summary

This chapter has highlighted the situation of intelligent children with specific language disability.   Many with this problem are struggling in our classrooms today.   Among them are fine minds, some ranging into the gifted class.   Often they excel in mathematics and science— superior thinkers whose intellectual capabilities are in the greatest demand.   Their problems are preventable if they are identified early and taught in a way that is right for them.

Although there is disagreement about the basic reasons for the different ways in which these children's minds function physiologically from the minds of those children who have experienced little difficulty in learning to read and spell, there is much agreement regarding the ways in which these children indicate that these differences exist.   That is, they show a difficulty in right-left orientation, difficulty in auditory and visual perception, difficulty in the Gestalt function.   (See footnote 22.)   In short, these children are different, and therefore it would seem should be taught in a different fashion; what is sauce for the goose is not always sauce for the gander.   The Gillingham, the Fernald, the

_____

80. Ibid., pp. 45-49.

Borel-Maisonny, the Norrie techniques take those differences into account and attempt to meet the children's requirements.*

There is widespread medical and educational agreement on the effectiveness of the Gillingham teaching techniques, or proper adaptations of them, as a remedy for the problem. The influence of these techniques is far reaching because the procedures are based on principles of neurophysiological functioning. And these principles of neurophysiological functioning suggest much broader teaching applications than those for specific language disability only.

Addendum

(a) The Gillingham-Stillman Manual (see pp. 19, 25, 26, 39), (b) the Slingerland-Gillingham materials (see p. 22), and (c) the Childs' current spelling publication (see p. 29) now may be obtained from the Educators Publishing Service, 301 Vassar Street, Cambridge, Massachusetts.

---

* A study of outstanding consequence was published (1962) by The Johns Hopkins Press, Baltimore, Md.: Reading Disability: Progress and Research Needs in Dyslexia, edited by John Money. This is a collection of thirteen papers presented at a conference at the Johns Hopkins Medical Institutions, Nov. 15-17, 1961. These papers represent lines of research that educators should pay attention to. The chapter by John Money reviews the conference itself, and in one short, important paragraph he specifies further needed research in dyslexia.

Also, two promising research projects are being undertaken in England at the Word Blind Centre for Dyslexic Children. They are entitled, "A Psycho-Neurological Research into the Aetiology of Specific Developmental Dyslexia in Children," and "The Evaluation of Remedial Techniques for Use with Dyslexic Children." Reference: Alex Bannatyne, B.A., Ph.D., "Research Needs in Dyslexia," Word Blind Committee Bulletin, Vol. I, No. 4, Winter 1964/1965, pp. 5-7 (published by Invalid Children's Aid Association Word Blind Committee, London, England).

CHAPTER II

SOME PERTINENT PSYCHOLOGICAL AND NEUROPHYSIOLOGICAL
ASPECTS OF LEARNING

Planning That Makes Interrelated Use of the Sensory-Motor Avenues
of Learning

Let me make clear the relationship between this chapter and the
first one. On page 42 the comment is that teaching procedures based on
principles of neurophysiological functioning suggest much broader teaching
applications than those for specific language disability only. As a means
of meeting the variety of individual learning differences in the classroom
it would seem possible that general public education, too, would benefit
from wider experimentation with carefully planned simultaneous or interrelated sensory-motor approaches. It is the aim in this chapter to present
psychological and neurophysiological backgrounds for this point of view.

We have seen how the type of language problem exhibited by specific
language disability children emphasized the necessity for specially planned
teaching procedures to assure the integrated or interrelated use of visual,
auditory, and kinesthetic learnings for phonograms, syllables, and words.
It will be remembered that certain combinations of the processes (A-K,
V-A, A-K, etc.) were linked in order to establish the associative welding
needed to build successful language function. The next step is to apply
widely--for any lesson presentation-- these neurophysiological principles
of establishing associations (through sensory-motor integration).

Thus, the practice of employing interrelationships among sensory-
motor approaches may be used as a criterion by the teacher. This means,
for instance, if teaching spelling, that he asks himself: "Have I made use
of all the ways, and combinations of ways, for the children to see the word,

43

to hear the word while they look (as I write at the chalkboard, building it up in sound and syllable), and to do (to write and speak the word with me as together we analyze the chalkboard copy of it and apply it in meaningful context)? Have I provided ways to call up all these verbal imageries simultaneously or in an interrelated way?"

If he has fulfilled this requirement, associated language linkages should stand a good chance of being built and strengthened in a greater number of his pupils.

The teacher has another reason for utilizing all the sensory-motor avenues. The reason has to do with imagery. Of the "two worlds--the world of perception and the world of imagery"[1]--imagery is discussed first.

In the general population there is much individual variation in types and combinations of recall imagery,[2] an activity which means simply this --remembering such matters as events, or objects, or words.[3] Plainly, the consideration of individual differences in recall imagery becomes important in any lesson planning--regardless of the subject.[4] Take an arithmetic process, for example. A pupil who has been exposed through films and chalkboard demonstration to an audio-visual explanation of re-lationships of fraction parts (4ths, 8ths, 16ths) may struggle over the process with pencil and paper. It is common knowledge among teachers, however, that for some children seeing, hearing, and speaking must be

---

1. Edwin G. Boring, Herbert S. Langfeld, and Harry P. Weld (editors), Foundations of Pyschology, John Wiley & Sons, Inc., New York, N.Y., 1948, p. 188.
    2. "Accurate recollection of the same object or event does not necessarily always take the same form. There are different kinds of recollection. One man may differ from another in the kind of recollection he uses most of the time. One task may differ from another in the type of recollection that is best suited to it. These differences are found between persons and also between recollections by the same person." Ibid., p. 194 (quoted with the permission of John Wiley & Sons, Inc.).
    3. Definitions--
        Recall: "To remember by recognition, recollection, or reinstatement (cf. remembering)."
        Image: "A recalled or imagined experience of perceptionlike qualities, whether visual, tactual, auditory, olfactory, gustatory, or kinesthetic without the presence of stimuli appropriate to these sensory experiences." Ernest R. Hilgard, Introduction to Psychology, Harcourt, Brace & World, Inc., New York, N.Y., 1953, pp. 607, 599.
    4. "We find great individual differences in types of recall image." From Remedial Techniques in Basic School Subjects, by Grace M. Fernald, p. 182. Copy-right, 1943. McGraw-Hill Book Co., New York, N.Y. Used by permission.

reinforced with the concrete kinesthetic experience of handling and moving the individual parts. For this purpose, wooden, felt, plastic, or paper fraction parts do wonders! The pupil must handle, he must manipulate the

 pieces. Through this activity, and perhaps through the <u>feel</u> of the pieces, he <u>helps</u> <u>him</u>-self to establish a mental concept--one strong enough to support retention in his memory. Now the fraction process be-gins to have some real meaning for him.[5]

Exactly what is it that finally gives events, or objects, or words, meaning to the individual? Besides interest, it is hard to say; it is differ-ent for different individuals. Thinking a moment about the example of the fraction parts, we know that association for remembrance is built not only

---

5. To cite another example: Interrelated activation of sensory-motor avenues and imagery may be practiced when introducing designated phonograms. The pro-cedure may be initiated by using a prepared series of key-word picture cards, organized to cover the different phonetic principles. For instance: the following sample card for the blend "pl" was made to incorporate ideas from Gillingham, Fernald, and Montessori.

Front of key word card   Back of key word card

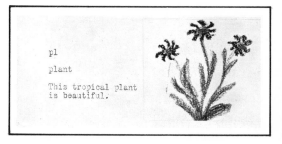

Consonant cards   Word in large cursive
(<u>blue</u> background)   writing may be traced,
                                if necessary.
Vowel cards
(<u>red</u> background)

Showing the card, the teacher says the sound "pl" and the word "plant" as she writes them on the chalkboard. Pupils needing this help do the same orally as they analyze the parts and the whole with her. Next, erasing the writing, she speaks the sound and the word; the children spell softly and write both phonogram and word. (See also Gillingham Manual for spelling techniques, Sixth edition, pp. 52-54.) The writing is a <u>doing</u> activity assisting association for sound and symbol—a kind of manipulative experience in verbal learning.

Each child's written work should be kept in organized form in a special notebook for this purpose.

Blackboards help learning. The boy at the far left is learning his new words by saying, seeing, hearing, and feeling—all simultaneously.

by using visual, auditory, and kinesthetic pathways in relation to one another, but by introducing through the senses, too, a multitude of helpers—color, rhythm, art, music, poetry, motion, texture, weight, machinery—to name only a few. Such as these add to meaning by serving the senses and imagery, too.

The principle of motivation is built strongly into our educational philosophy. We believe thoroughly in the value of trying to interest the student. We know, too, that approval is powerful reinforcement for stimulating learning. Along with these principles, could we not incorporate into our thinking an additional principle, one of planning that makes integrated use of the sensory-motor approach? All good teachers do use a variety of approaches, and do use visual, auditory, and kinesthetic pathways, but what I am stressing is:

(1) That in preparing lessons the kind of planning which is consciously organized to use all the pathways, either in interrelationship or simultaneously, makes active provision for building and strengthening the sensory-motor "linkages."

46

(2) That this application of planning to relate the sensory-motor pathways could eventually become as familiar to us as are the ideas of motivation and the reinforcing of children's efforts through approval.

(3) That a significant aspect of planning is concerned with providing for individual differences in recall imagery.

(4) That how the sensory-motor avenues are to be used to care for imagery differences in the classroom calls for imagination.

In the remaining sections of this chapter we give attention to enlightening excerpts from reports in psychology, art education, physiology, and neurology.

Imagery

It would seem appropriate at this time to talk more fully about imagery.

Early work in the field of imagery was done by Francis Galton in 1883. He established the fact that among individuals there are great differences in memory images. As a result of his experiments, a theory of imagery types was developed. This theory held that a person learned by a visual, an auditory, or a motor means.[6]

Subsequent experimentation, however, revealed that such matters are not usually so distinctly compartmentalized. According to Fernald, most individuals recall objects, for instance, with a mixed type of imagery,[7] perhaps auditory and visual, or kinesthetic and visual. Thus, while it is difficult to make a general statement on imagery, most persons use different imageries, all types perhaps—depending on the occasion. For example:

> If you can see the Mona Lisa in your "mind's eye," you can
> do a good job at recollecting it. If you have to depend on

6. Robert S. Woodworth, Psychology, Henry Holt and Company, New York, N.Y., third edition, 1936, pp. 31-32.

7. Grace M. Fernald, Remedial Techniques in Basic School Subjects, McGraw-Hill Book Co., New York, N.Y., 1943, p. 319.

kinesthesis, you will be likely to get only the words with which you originally described it. On the other hand, if you are remembering the Ninth Symphony, auditory imagery is more fun, even though visual recollection of the looks of the score may be quite accurate.[8]

Referring to Fernald again, she believed that although educators have placed great importance on visual recall, there is evidence that "many persons do their most accurate and detailed thinking in nonvisual terms." [9] [10] [11]

Another investigator in the area of imagery is the art educator, Viktor Lowenfeld. His findings show that there are two extreme creative types, which he labels visual and haptic (meaning "able to lay hold of," from the Greek word haptikos and explained in the next quotation). He makes clear that the majority of persons fall between the two extremes.[12] Excerpts from his discussion of the development of these two creative types are as follows:

> We can now clearly distinguish two types of art expression both by the end product and by the attitude toward experience. When we investigate the artistic products of these two types in their pure forms we find that the visual type starts from his

8. Edwin G. Boring, Herbert S. Langfeld, and Harry P. Weld (editors), Foundations of Psychology, John Wiley & Sons, Inc., New York, N.Y., 1948, p. 194. Quoted with the permission of the publishers.

9. From Remedial Techniques in Basic School Subjects, by Grace M. Fernald, p. 319. Copyright, 1943. McGraw-Hill Book Co., New York, N.Y. Used by permission.

10. Fernald has interesting material abstracted from biographies on individual differences in learning. Included in brief descriptions are such men as: A. Binet, Auguste Rodin, William James, Robert Louis Stevenson, Thomas Edison, and Leonardo da Vinci. In this same section, Galton is quoted as saying that "scientific men as a class have feeble powers of visual representation." She also has a section in the Appendix entitled "Individual Differences in Imagery." In this section are several Imagery Tests and reference to a monograph by M. R. Fernald, "Diagnosis of Mental Imagery," Psychol. Monogr., 14, Feb., 1912. See Ibid., pp. 172-175, 319-322.

11. Re: imagery—"People differ enormously in the richness of their imagery." On Galton's findings regarding deficiency in imagery of most scientists: "These findings show us that richness of thinking does not depend solely upon richness of imagery." Ernest R. Hilgard, Introduction to Psychology, Harcourt, Brace & World, Inc., New York, N. Y., 1953, p. 320.

12. "While I have emphasized again and again that visual and nonvisual forms of art expression lie on a continuum, and that 'most individuals fall between the extremes, with a preference toward one or the other,' and with overlappings of both, distorted reference to the mere existence of pure types has been made by some teachers and writers." Reprinted with the permission of the publisher from Creative and Mental Growth, by Viktor Lowenfeld, p. xi. Copyright 1957 by The Macmillan Company, New York, N.Y.

environment, that he feels as spectator, and that his inter-
mediaries for experience are mainly the eyes. The other,
which we shall call the haptic type, is primarily concerned
with his own body sensations and the subjective experiences
in which he feels emotionally involved. In The Nature of
Creative Activity I have demonstrated the existence of these
two distinct creative types based upon two different reactions
toward the world of experiences. . . .

A visually minded individual would be disturbed and
inhibited were he to be stimulated only by means of haptic
impressions— that is, were he asked not to use sight, but
to orientate himself only by means of touch, bodily feelings,
muscular sensations, and kinesthetic fusions. So much is
clear, but what is not as obvious is that "seeing" may also
become an inhibitory factor when forced upon an individual
who does not use his visual experiences for creative work.
Both facts are established by numerous experiments reported in the work referred to before.

An extreme haptical type of individual—who is by no
means rare— is normal-sighted and uses his eyes only when
compelled to do so; otherwise he reacts as would a blind
person who is entirely dependent upon touch and kinesthesis. . . .

Most people fall between these two extreme types.
Investigations have proved, however, that only a few individuals
have equal amounts of visual and haptic predisposition.
Seventy-five per cent have an appreciable tendency toward
one or the other . . . . the tendency toward these two antip-
odes of experience is important not only for the proper
stimulation in creative activity but also to life in general
(especially, in the proper choice of occupation) . . .

The result of an investigation in which I tested 1128
subjects by means of specifically designed tests for visual
or haptic aptitude was as follows: 47 per cent were clearly
visual, 23 per cent were haptic, and 30 per cent either re-
ceived a score below the line where a clear identification
was possible, or were otherwise not identifiable. In other
words, approximately half of the individuals tested reacted
visually, whereas not quite a fourth reacted haptically.
These figures completely coincide with those of W. Grey
Walter in his entirely independent study. [See p. 50.]

Thus, it would appear that one among four individuals
depends more on his subjective reactions such as touch and
kinesthesis than upon vision. Aside from its far-reaching
significance in other fields, for art teaching this fact means
that only half of the population can benefit from visual
stimuli. The others either are not reached or may become
frustrated by this type of stimulation. Each type should
therefore be stimulated in the direction of his experiences

and thinking. To do this, we should become acquainted with the nature of these two creative types, particularly because during the crisis of adolescence the individual is most unsure of himself. The kind of stimulation that is able to inspire him will not only contribute to his creative development, but will also instill the self-confidence necessary for a wholesome personality development. In spite of the fact that most people fall between the two types, with merely a preference for the one or the other, an analysis of each type in its pure form seems imperative for the proper understanding of their "mixed" forms.[13]

Does not this awareness of imagery differences, this wise philosophy of planning for them, make this passage significant for education in general as well as for art education?

Addendum

W. Grey Walter, to whom Lowenfeld refers, is a distinguished physiologist at the Burden Neurological Institute, Bristol, England. He has made extensive studies of brain waves (electroencephalography) which are reported in his book, The Living Brain.[14] To make a capsule-like statement concerning this complicated subject: the findings of Walter and his associates "suggested that the amount, voltage and responsiveness of alpha rhythm [the predominant cortical rhythm in adults] may be used as an indicator of habitual mental imagery. . . . "[15]

In his book Walter classifies the electroencephalograph tracings of the alpha rhythm as follows:

13. Ibid., pp. 262-264. Reprinted with the permission of the publisher; copyright 1957 by the Macmillan Company, New York, N.Y.
14. W. Grey Walter, The Living Brain, W. W. Norton & Company, Inc., New York, N.Y., 1953.
15. A. C. Mundy-Castle, "An Appraisal of Electroencephalography in Relation to Psychology," Journal of the National Institute for Personnel Research, Monograph Supplement No. 2, May, 1958, p. 3.

P Group	M Group	R Group

In the P group (P is for "persistent") alpha rhythms are persistent and difficult to "block with mental effort."

Persons in this group "tend to auditory, kinesthetic or tactile perceptions rather than visual imagery."[16]

In the M group (M is for "minus") no alpha rhythms of consequence show up in the EEG (electroencephalogram) even when the eyes are closed and the mind unoccupied.

Persons in this group are those "whose thinking processes are conducted almost entirely in terms of visual imagery." [17]

In the R group (R is for "responsive") the alpha rhythms are spoken of as "responsive."

Persons in this group "are intermediate between the other two groups;" their "alpha rhythms disappear" when they do mental arithmetic or have their eyes open; they may or may not use mental pictures for ordinary thinking; and they "can combine data from the various sense organs more readily than can either the M or P types."

Groups studied indicated that in general the R type made up about two-thirds of the subjects. The other third was approximately evenly distributed between the M and P types.[18]

He points out that these differences in imagery would appear to explain the differences in thinking of three different personality groups. He states that evidence "both statistical and experimental, strongly suggests that the alpha rhythm characteristics are inborn and probably hereditary."[19]

---

16. W. Grey Walter, The Living Brain, W. W. Norton & Company, Inc., New York, N.Y., 1953, p. 214.
17. Ibid., p. 215.
18. Ibid., pp. 214, 216, 217.
19. Ibid., p. 218.

Unaccepting of these findings concerning alpha rhythm and imagery is an appraisal by Mundy-Castle. In the aforementioned monograph he states that "The consensus of opinion appears to be that there is no simple, one-to-one relationship between alpha type and imagery . . . that alpha blocking is not necessarily evidence of visualization. It is therefore untrue to state that the behaviour of the alpha rhythm provides a reliable, objective measure of mental imagery."[20]

I am not qualified to judge the validity of either the imagery investigation or the refutation. Nevertheless, the observations on mental imagery are of significance to the educator, and it has seemed important to include this brief summary of Walter's findings because of Lowenfeld's statement that his own figures "completely coincide with those of W. Grey Walter in his entirely independent study."[21]

Examples of Recall Imagery--Two Kinds

This section is meant to make clear two kinds of recollection (or imagery) with which the classroom teacher deals very specifically every

20. A. C. Mundy-Castle, "An Appraisal of Electroencephalography in Relation to Psychology," Journal of the National Institute for Personnel Research, Monograph Supplement No. 2, May, 1958, p. 3.
The following description given by Walter Friedlander, M.D., Chief, National Veteran's Epilepsy Center, Veterans Administration Hospital, Boston, Mass., may help the reader to follow Mundy-Castle's discussion: "Alpha is a regular sinusoidal rhythm which is usually, although not invariably obtained when the subject is sitting with his eyes closed. When he opens his eyes, this electrical rhythm suddenly changes from the regular sinusoidal pattern to a low voltage, fast, electrical pattern; it is this that is referred to as 'blocking.' 'Blocking' is probably not due to opening the eyes and 'seeing' but rather to the subject's attempt at visualization or thinking. A similar 'blocking' can occur with the eyes closed and the subject given an arithmetic problem to concentrate on; or if he opens his eyes in a totally darkened room, there will be 'blocking' —not as a result of his seeing anything, but as a result of his searching around in an attempt to see something. 'Blocking' implies the stoppage of something and, indeed, the alpha is stopped. But this stoppage actually is the result of change in nervous function, not a decrease in nervous function. Alpha represents a synchronization of nerve cell discharge, whereas the low voltage, fast pattern seen when the alpha is 'blocked' is due to a desynchronization of nerve cell discharge. This desynchronization is probably brought about by an alerting response of the reticular formation [a network of cells and fibers in a region of the brainstem]." Letter, Mar. 23, 1961.
21. Reprinted with the permission of the publisher from Creative and Mental Growth, by Viktor Lowenfeld, p. 263. Copyright 1957 by The Macmillan Company, New York, N.Y.

day. The distinction to be made is between concrete imagery and verbal imagery.[22]

Concrete imagery concerns recall resulting from perceptual experiences with objects (direct learning).[23] Verbal imagery concerns recall resulting from perceptual experiences with symbols that stand for objects —and for ideas, too, (indirect learning). In other words, one learning is concrete; the other is abstract.

When it comes to memory or recall, object memory is for the concrete object and verbal memory is for the abstraction (verbal symbols). It is important to know that a person may have good visual memory for objects but poor visual memory for recognition of words. For example, a boy may be able to recall visually how a certain piece of machinery looks, how the parts fit together, and how they function, but he may have difficulty with visual recognition and recall of words.

It is possible, then, that a person may have, for instance,

1. (a) Good visual memory or recall for objects, and

    (b) Poor visual memory or recall for words (as in reading), or for reproduction of words (as in spelling)

2. (a) Good auditory memory or recall for repeating sentences or stories, and

    (b) Poor auditory memory or recall for repeating individual sounds (as, ĭ for ĕ in speech), or for being able to reproduce individual sounds, blends, or syllables (as in written spelling)

It is also important to remember that most persons have mixed combinations of recall imagery. In the case of verbal recall for the word "hammer," an individual may see what it looks like in print and hear it

---

22. The terms "concrete" and "verbal" are used by Edwin G. Boring, Herbert S. Langfeld, and Harry P. Weld (editors), Foundations of Psychology, John Wiley & Sons, Inc., New York, N.Y., 1943, p. 194.
23. It is to be understood that perceptual experiences in this sense refer to more than mere sensory stimuli. They refer also to recognition and meaning. This distinction is made because a person can look at an object or a word and not necessarily register recognition or meaning.

spoken; or if he wishes to write it, he may have to sound it out or spell it softly to himself.

For purposes of clarity, the following chart has been constructed. It illustrates the distinction between concrete imagery and verbal imagery. Much of the chart was suggested by material in Foundations of Psychology. The example used in this reference is a hammer, and the same example is used here. A second reference for the chart is The Thinking Body.[24]

Visual Perception—Differences in "Types" and Range of Abilities and in " 'Types' of Perceivers"[25]

Referring to a previous quotation, we now turn from the "world of imagery" to "the world of perception."[26] In this instance, as explained previously, perception includes recognition and meaning as well as sensory stimuli, and the particular perception to be considered is visual perception.

Jean Turner Goins has investigated the "relation of visual perception to progress in reading in the first grade . . ."[27] As a brief report on certain phases of her study, it may be said that the results of the investigation seemed to verify the following two hypotheses:

1. "That selected tests of visual perception will reveal various types of perceptual abilities and degrees of competence and will also delineate 'types' of perceivers."

2. "That the results of this testing will show significant correlations with later success in reading."[28]

---

24. Edwin G. Boring, Herbert S. Langfeld, and Harry P. Weld (editors), Foundations of Psychology, John Wiley & Sons, Inc., New York, N.Y., 1948, p. 194. Mabel Ellsworth Todd, The Thinking Body, Charles T. Branford Co., Boston, Mass., 1949, pp. 6-7, 26-28.
25. Jean Turner Goins, Visual Perceptual Abilities and Early Reading Progress, University of Chicago Press, Supplementary Educational Monographs, Number 87, Feb., 1958, p. 4. Copyright 1958 by The University of Chicago.
26. Edwin G. Boring, Herbert S. Langfeld, and Harry P. Weld, Foundations of Psychology, (editors), John Wiley & Sons, Inc., New York, N.Y., 1948, p. 188.
27. Jean Turner Goins, Visual Perceptual Abilities and Early Reading Progress, University of Chicago Press, Supplementary Educational Monographs, Number 87, Feb., 1958, p. 1. Copyright 1958 by The University of Chicago.
28. Ibid., p. 4.

Two types of perceptual ability, as shown by the tests and a "theoretical interpretation" for effectual reading are:

1. The "ability to perceive and to keep in mind a perceptual whole."[29] (For example, applying this idea, translate "whole" to mean a word, a phrase, or a sentence.)

2. The ability "to hold in mind a whole . . . while at the same time he manipulates in some way the 'parts' of the whole."[30] (For example, applying this idea, again translate "whole" to mean a word, a phrase, or a sentence; and translate " 'parts' of the whole" to mean the integral parts of each.)[31]

The study also identified two "types of perceivers," who varied in their methods of "attacking the same perceptual task."[32] For example, it was noted that children examining a picture square (made up of nine small pictures, three pictures to a row, and only two of the nine being exactly alike) used the following methods of attack:

1. Some children looked at the picture square as "a whole" and quickly identified the two like pictures. (Progress with the test was rapid.)

2. Some children looked at each picture individually and in an orderly sequence, and attempted to use a matching technique until the two like pictures were found. (Progress with the test was slow.)

The author did not make final conclusions regarding reading failure, but her results permitted her to conclude that "the superior readers are shown to be a 'type of perceiver' different from the type of the poorer readers."[33]

---

29. Ibid., p. 102.
30. Ibid., p. 104.
31. The author believes the results of her study suggest a need for including in reading-readiness tests, tests that measure this latter named ability. She says: "Batteries of reading-readiness tests already utilize tests that measure the first factor revealed by the present analysis, namely, ability to perceive and to keep in mind a perceptual whole. These tests have formerly been called 'speed of perception' tests. On the basis of the evidence secured in this investigation, tests measuring strength of closure [the ability to manipulate parts of the whole while keeping in mind the whole] should also be included." Ibid., p. 102.
32. Ibid.
33. Ibid. The Picture Squares test scores and the reading scores taken on the same selected first grade pupils showed a "fairly high correlation." The children with the superior scores on the timed Picture Squares test made the higher scores in reading achievement, too.

In her opinion,

> The implications of . . . findings for the teaching of reading are similar to those resulting from our present knowledge that some children are visual and some are auditory learners. Both types benefit when beginning teaching methods make use of both sight and sound techniques. If types of perceivers can be isolated, it may be that varying methods of teaching can be developed to fit the needs of different types, which will result in more efficient learning at this level. Also those pupils who are likely to experience some perceptual interferences may be identified at an early date by the results of tests in the visual perceptual domain.[34]

It should be remarked that in order to protect the results of the study from merely distinguishing the readers from the non-readers, the only tests used were nonverbal (pictures). These were carefully chosen by recognized authorities in the fields of reading and psychology. The children to be tested were first-graders— since one aspect of the matter being investigated was the relation of visual perception to beginning reading success.

Because an interpretation of relationships of visual perception to the reading process has so much meaning for those who are concerned with prevention of early reading failure, and because a few tests may hold promise for a fairly simple means of determining visual perceptual differences and " 'types' of perceivers," it would seem that a direct quotation from this monograph might be of the greatest value. Therefore, an excerpt concerning these matters is given:

Relation of Visual Perception to Reading

> . . .an attempt is made to set forth a theoretical interpretation of the nature of the visual perceptual process revealed by this study and by similar studies and its relationship to the process of learning to read.
>
> Since the turn of the century, when experimental investigations revealed that the unit of recognition in reading was the word and groups of words rather than individual letters comprising words, there has been considerable interest in the nature of visual perception in reading. Changes in reading methodology during the last fifty years have reflected the changing concepts of the nature

---

34. Ibid., pp. 102-103.

of visual perception involved in the reading act. Early reports emphasized the value of teaching children to read by "wholes"--directing attention in turn to the story, the paragraph, the sentence, and the word. Prior to this period, analytical methods had been based on a system ascending from letters to syllables to words. Modern European investigators are currently concerned with the evaluation of whole versus part methods of teaching word perception. However, it has become increasingly clear, as the approach to reading through emphasis upon wholes has become almost universally adopted, that certain pupils do not make satisfactory progress in learning to read when instruction directs attention solely to word wholes.

Based on the evidence of the present study, a theory of the nature of visual perception in reading is postulated thus: Efficient reading involves ability not only to hold in mind the "wholeness" of a word, phrase, or sentence (that is, to perceive its larger relationships both mechanically and ideationally) but also to attend to individual words and, at times, to parts of words. Perceiving in a general way the whole but not discriminating clearly among its component elements (letters, words, phrases) may cause as much difficulty in reading as does concentrated attention on word-analysis and word-calling. The good reader either develops or possesses inherently strength of closure, thus performing both acts in harmony or simultaneously.

It appears that six relatively simple tests of visual perception used in this study may ascertain early and easily the type of pupil who is able to take advantage of modern methods of learning to read. Conversely, the tests may identify those pupils requiring other types of instruction. These six perceptual tests, which measure the second factor, are: 1, Pictures; 3, Picture Squares; 9, Pattern Completion; 10, Pattern Copying; 11, Figures; and 12, Reversals. These tests appear to measure a type of strength of closure that can best be described as requiring the subject to hold in mind a whole, a perceptual Gestalt, while at the same time he manipulates in some way the "parts" of the whole.[35]

Brain Function and Education

Finally now, before concluding this journey through some pertinent psychological and neurophysiological aspects of learning, we come to one more exploration—one intended to impress on us that research on brain function has application for education.

How does the brain integrate or unify the thousands of varied sensory

---

35. Ibid., pp. 103-104.

stimuli that assail it? How does it choose among myriad possibilities
what it will do now or what it may decide to do later?

What attention-getting device focused meaning and aroused fourteen-
year-old John's absorbing interest in ancient history? Why did it take
the responsibility of a construction job to give meaning and to provide at
last a way for Warren, a boy with no rote memory, to remember his
multiplication tables? What means to engage attention, to sharpen perception, and to improve memory might have helped him while he was still in
school? Some answers to this last question may be suggested by recent
neurophysiological investigation of brain function.

Today, certain major investigations of brain function are based on a
promising theory developed and popularized by Wilder Penfield, neurosur-
geon of the Montreal Neurological Institute at McGill University.[36]

Briefly, the theory proposes that the integrating, unifying, choosing
process which goes on in the brain is "achieved by a complex inter-
change of nerve impulses—bearing coded information" between nerve
cells in the cortex (the "outer bark") of the brain, and nerve cells in a
region of the brainstem known as the reticular formation.[37] [38] It is
hypothesized that the "reticular system acts as integrating mechanism for
incoming, outgoing, and reverberating signals [stimuli]";[39] that it is involved
in arousal, attention, sorting; that it is "in a unique position to monitor all
incoming sensory messages";[40] and that the cortex, on the other hand, gives

36. "... Dr. Penfield described a principle of cerebral organization, implying
from considerable evidence obtained from stimulation and lesion experiments, or
observations in man, things which forced him to the conclusion that there must be
a central integrating system, and that the cortex was a relay to this system."
Herbert H. Jasper and Others (editors), Henry Ford Hospital International Symposium, Reticular Formation of the Brain, Little, Brown and Company, Boston, Mass.,
1958, p. 506.
37. Francis Bello, "New Light on the Brain," in the Editors of Fortune, The
Mighty Force of Research, McGraw-Hill Book Co., New York, N.Y., 1956, p. 89.
38. "The reticular formation or nerve net of the brainstem is a gateway to
the cortex. It 'clears' certain signals for top-level consideration." John Pfeiffer,
The Human Brain, Harper & Brothers, New York, N.Y., 1955, p. 73.
39. Walter Friedlander, M.D., Chief, National Veteran's Epilepsy Center,
Veterans Administration Hospital, Boston, Mass. Interview.
40. Donald B. Lindsley, "The Reticular System and Perceptual Discrimination," in Jasper and Others (editors), Henry Ford Hospital International Symposium,
Reticular Formation of the Brain, Little, Brown and Company, Boston, Mass., 1958,
p. 519.

precise meanings to what we see, hear, touch, taste, and smell, and that it serves as a storehouse for these meanings.[41]   The inference is that "final integration" of sensory information in the reticular system results in selected impulses (stimuli) to the cortex which, because of especial importance to our interests in this book, includes the sensorimotor cortex. The cortex, in turn, probably determines the type of resultant behavior, or perhaps thought.[42]   Let me illustrate.   A mother, through a barrage of television noise, conversation, and a jet whizzing overhead, hears her baby crying in the next room. This cry is the sound above all others that is "monitored" or sorted out as having immediate meaning for her.

For purposes of clarity, the diagrammatic representation of the idea of brain systems is inserted on the following page. Here, the inference is that we all have these connections anatomically, but that they may function differently in different persons.

The diagram is intended to stress the idea of interacting systems. IT IS NOT INTENDED TO SUGGEST LOCALIZATION OF AREAS OF AUDITION, VISION, KINESTHESIS, AND THE RETICULAR SYSTEM.

Dr. Penfield says:

"And where is the place of understanding?"
· · · the integrating circuits, without which there can be no conscious processes of the mind, are to be found deep within the cerebral hemispheres.

. . . I have spoken vaguely of a hypothetical integrating system and have given it the name centrencephalic for purposes of convenience. But recent studies . . . give us direct evidence concerning the functional activity of this system.

. . . the circuits of this system run out to the various functional areas of the cortex and back again. The memory cortex forms one of these areas. . . . The "place of understanding"

---

41. "The demonstration of the existence of cortical 'patterns' that preserve the detail of current experience, as though in a library of many volumes, is one of the first steps toward a physiology of the mind. The nature of the pattern, the mechanism of its formation, the mechanism of its subsequent utilization, and the integrative processes that form the substratum of consciousness—these will one day be translated into physiological formulas." Wilder Penfield, M.D., "Memory Mechanisms," A.M.A. Archives of Neurology and Psychiatry, Vol. 67, No. 2, Feb., 1952, p. 191.

42. Francis Bello, "New Light on the Brain," in The Editors of Fortune, The Mighty Force of Research, McGraw-Hill Book Co., New York, N.Y., 1956, p. 89.

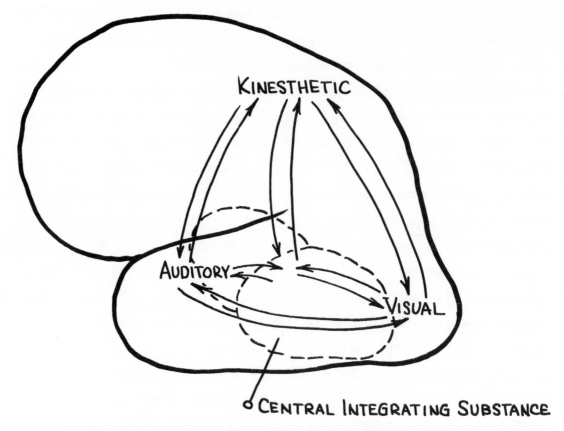

Inferences re Integrative Systems (Schematic)

is not walled up in a cell or in a center of gray matter. It is to be
sought in the perfect functioning of all these converging circuits.
        . . . The system does not function by itself. It functions to-
gether with all the other areas--cortex and other parts of the
central nervous system. Thus, when it is functioning, all parts
of the brain that are needed for that particular function come
into action.[43]

To mention another example which illustrates response, there is an

interesting account by Hermann of his analysis of the reading act. It is

his idea that the "functions [in the process of reading, or in the process

of writing] are integrated so closely that they proceed simultaneously."[44]

However, as an aid to pinpointing disturbance of function, of locating which

part of the integrative function has broken down, he has constructed a four-

        43.   Wilder Penfield, M.D., "Memory Mechanisms," A.M.A. Archives of
Neurology and Psychiatry, Vol. 67, No. 2, Feb., 1952, pp. 178, 191, 198.
        44.   Knud Hermann, M.D., Reading Disability, Charles C Thomas, Springfield,
Ill., 1959, p. 51 (with the permission of the original publisher, Munksgaard A/S,
Copenhagen).

stage "schematic" description of the reading act. He does the same for the writing process. It is his belief that "this approach may possibly lead one to conclusions about the activity of the normal functions of reading and writing, and this may conceivably have a bearing not only on the special education of the word-blind, but also on the education of normal pupils."[45][46]

This consideration of so complex a subject as brain function is not intended to be finely detailed. Its major purpose has been to emphasize the existence of continuing investigations which ultimately should help clarify the mechanisms of such abstract functions as perception, learning, and memory. At this writing we can conclude that the higher functions of the brain are carried out by interacting systems; and that, with increased understanding of neurophysiological function, more precise interpretation of psychological observations may ensue. Because we would expect such discoveries to have many real implications for teaching, we guard against becoming static in our approaches to learning and await new developments with anticipation.

Meanwhile, how will present knowledge of brain function help teaching? Although this knowledge is incomplete and what is known is difficult for the layman to understand, the implications for teaching are unmistakable. We recall the inference that resultant behavior and perhaps thought may be determined by what happens in the brain to "selected" stimuli from sensory input. Bearing this inference in mind, then how and with what

---

45. Ibid.
46. Ibid., pp. 41, 42. Description of the four stages of the reading act:
   1. "Perception of written characters as letters, i.e. recognition of a series of figures as being symbols which represent a system of sounds—a purely figural recognition.
   2. "The connection between the outline of the letter and its associated sound; in this part of the process, the letter's nominal designation (as in the alphabet) must must be replaced by the language sound which the letter represents in the word concerned—except in the case of a phonetic script. By virtue of its function in the word, the individual letter symbol may have a phonetic value which is wholly differ- ent from its designation in the alphabet, and which can change according to the constellation of letters in which it occurs.
   3. "The letters are integrated, as representatives of language sounds, into a word symbol.
   4. "For the meaning to emerge, the words must be comprehended as the entity which the sentence constitutes. . . . "

61

we activate the sensory and motor avenues seems important in teaching. It is true that we do not have enough knowledge to predict which sensory information will be "selected" as meaningful in the brain of a given individual. Nevertheless, it seems reasonable to speculate that simultaneous or interrelated stimulation of sight, sound, and kinesthesis would provide this individual with wider opportunity for "selection" of information. Therefore, related information made available through eyes, ears, and hands, accompanied by motor activity through voice, hands, or body movement, should increase the chances of improving perception, learning, and memory in each one. For instance, there is the case of John, a specific language disability boy, originally severely handicapped in reading, who finally learned to read— but not to spell. It was the film "Helen of Troy" that triggered his interest in Greek history—an interest which eventually carried him into the Histories of Herodotus. Initial "selection" for him was through simultaneous audio-visual stimulation. For Holly, a highly verbal child with superior reading ability, original interest in the same subject was inspired by reading the Greek myths and by personal dramatic involvement. Initial "selection" here was through books and reading, supported later by motor expression (dramatics)—a combination of both verbal and concrete experience.

Going back to John, the possibility is almost certain that he would have rejected Holly's beginning approach. But in each case the drama of the subject matter was what interested them. It was a question of finding the approach that could give meaning and arouse interest in each child.

At this point a review of several well-established principles is in order.

1. "Whenever what happens to an object is sensed in more than one way, the resulting perception is likely to be more complete and more sharply set off."[47]

---

47. Edwin G. Boring, Herbert S. Langfeld, and Harry P. Weld (editors), Foundations of Psychology, John Wiley & Sons, Inc., New York, N.Y., 1948, p. 229. Quoted with the permission of the publishers.

2. "The way we learn skilled acts illustrates how enduring traces may be formed. Such memory feeds on repetition. The more you practice the better you become, within limits."[48]

3. "The learner, for best results, must actually work with the real materials he is trying to learn to deal with. For example, typewriting is not taught by the lecture method . . ."[49]

Obviously these principles underlie the generally accepted foundations of day-in-and-day-out teaching. Their validity is borne out by psychological and medical research and by empirical results already known to teachers. In considering both the language disabilities of the few and the diverse imageries of the classroom masses, the teacher's task becomes one of continuously applying the principles to verbal learnings as well as to concrete learnings. Ruch believes that "When the learning task becomes less tangible . . . educators still typically neglect the principle that efficient learning requires the opportunity to deal functionally with real materials."[50]

As will have been noted, this book stresses verbal skills of writing, reading, spelling, and speaking through an intensely specific application of the idea of simultaneous or interrelated stimulation of the sensory-motor pathways. The section on Montessori indicates the great extent to which this organic and functional approach can be applied in achieving language skills.[51]

---

48. John Pfeiffer, The Human Brain, Harper & Brothers, New York, N.Y., 1955, p. 80.
49. Floyd L. Ruch, Psychology and Life, third edition, Scott, Foresman and Company, Chicago, Ill., 1948, p. 342.
50. Ibid.
51. For those interested in further consideration of the specific area of brain research: a professional article, "Reticular Mechanisms and Behavior," by Ina Samuels, appears in the Psychological Bulletin, Vol. 56, No. 1, Jan., 1959, pp. 1-25.
References for two popular articles concerning Dr. Penfield's work are:
Wilder Penfield, "New Explorations of the Human Brain," Best Articles and Stories, Vol. IV, No. 1, Jan., 1960, pp. 27-31.
Murray Teigh Bloom, "Explorer of the Brain," The Elizabethan, Vol. 1, No. 2, June, 1958, pp. 26-28, 43.

The ideas presented in this entire chapter take into consideration that one human organism learns one way; that the next one learns another way. The approaches suggested here are rooted in psychological and neurophysiological research, and, even though so much in this area is undetermined, teaching practices can operate on the hypothesis of simultaneous or inter-related sensory-motor approach until a better theory is set forth. Everything about my personal experience in teaching supports this hypothesis.

CHAPTER III

THE CHILDREN: PART TWO

Children with Diverse Problems

Until now, the discussion has stressed the use of the neurophysiological approach for specific language disability children and a broader
application of its principles for the classroom masses.

Let us look now at some individual children with diverse problems.
Each child to be described was in a public school classroom preceding
his illness, and each returned to public school. All exhibited average
or better than average intelligence; and all but one exemplify a class
of children in our schools who are burdened with problems. In the cases
of these particular children, illness had been an added handicap.

At the time the following anecdotal-type notations were written, the
children were recovering in a convalescent home where they were at-
tending school in their respective wards. Like the one-room country
school, the ward classroom was a multi-graded, multi-problem situation,
with ages ranging from five to fifteen years.

It will be observed that the situations of all these children except
one were complicated by their personal difficulties. Undoubtedly, the
reader is well aware of the unfortunate and unhappy details commonly
found in the lives of many children. By deliberate intent, the specific
personal problems of these particular children have been minimized.
Instead, the attempt has been made to indicate and reveal needs through
a description of the children and their work rather than to recount and
venture explanations of their individual troubles. It is intended, too,
that the implications of the notations be both practical and useful, especially

for young teachers. In short—<u>how</u> the teacher meets some of the child's needs through the school program, and <u>what</u> she does, is considered to be of more significance to this book than explanations as to <u>why</u> the child is as he is.

Of course, the other components associated with "how" and "what" are the teacher's understanding of the individual's problems; the relation which she builds with each one; the feeling she helps to create in the group as a whole; and the realization that her best efforts may be limited by a child's need for family love and attention—which remains an unsolved problem for countless children in our society.

Just as the neurologist through his analysis of acquired disabilities has gained insight into normal function, so teachers dealing with individuals and small groups have been able to analyze learning procedures, and their experiences can light the way for use with larger groups.

I have known many children personally, and from my notebook the following five have been chosen for introduction.

I will begin with Keith.

Notations on These Children

Name: Keith D. (intense, active child)
Age: 9 years, 3 months
Grade: Low 4
Attendance: 4 months (at the time of this notation)

Personal Note

Keith lived with a foster family. In addition, he had an uncle for whom he seemed to have deep antagonisms, and an aunt who seemed to provide the most stable force in his life.

Reason for Presentation

The notation on Keith has been included to show (1) that even though a social-emotional disturbance coupled with physical impairment affects attitude and performance, some success in school does provide satisfaction and a kind of bulwark; (2) that art and music are essential parts of a school program; and (3) that more mental health facilities need to be available for our schools.

Observation and Comment on Keith

Keith was nervous, tense, and easily frustrated by school work or personal encounters. There were numerous incidents, such as scratching-up the letters he had written to his uncle, or gouging them full of holes; there were confidences, too, which exposed his fears of punishment. On occasion he was untruthful and tried to achieve his ends by devious means. His anger was very explosive, and his nervousness and tense state carried over into almost all phases of his work. It is important to say that he could be very appealing and that he had many likable qualities.

In this situation, the attempt was made to help him build strengths through successes in school, and through opportunities for practice of satisfying relationships. These measures were helpful, but his problem was far from being solved. It seemed evident that Keith needed not only individual psychological help, but also real security and understanding from someone close to him who cared.

Excerpts from School Progress Report (which was written at the end of four months' time)

"Keith has continued to make great gains in reading. He has become fluent; he reads in school and out; and he enjoys it tremendously. The ideas and pictures that he finds in books stimulate him and he will talk about them with the greatest interest and enthusiasm. In very clear language he can reproduce the substance of what he has been reading. He has been doing this exceptionally well lately in connection with science materials. Also, when social studies discussions come up, he may become highly excitable, but his thinking is excellent, and he contributes fine suggestions in group work.

"Written work is still quite cramped and does not come too easily. For this reason he has been practicing at a large chalkboard and does his writing in large size.

"Arithmetic is his Waterloo. He has disliked it heartily, and the problem has been to help him become more interested in working at it. In order to build concepts in all fundamental processes, it is important still to use a variety of objects for him to handle. He is behind grade in this work.

"Keith is easily upset if something he is doing doesn't go well, but he shows improvement in that he will eventually return to it.

"He requires time to experiment in music and in his art efforts. In art, when he finally thinks through his idea, he works very absorbedly and intensely. The results are often unusual and original, and his sense of color is spectacular. He loves music, and here again, he shows real imagination in his use of the percussion instruments."

Name: Sam A. (inactive, isolated child)

Age: 6 years, 11 months

Grade: High 1

Attendance: 5 months

Personal Note

Sam was troubled by what seemed to be lack of understanding from adults, and he was supposed to have demonstrated irritable, resistant behavior at home and at school.

Reason for Presentation

The notation on Sam has been included to show that it is helpful for teachers to know various remedial approaches to learning, and to provide the reader with a specific explanation of exactly what procedures were used in this instance.

Observation and Comment on Sam

Sam was large for his age, clumsy in all his movements, and rather untidy looking. He was quiet and showed no evidence of being a behavior problem. In both reading and writing he was completely confused, and he seemed unable to take initiative in anything. He did not play much with the other children—he watched them play.

Excerpts from School Progress Report (which was written at the end of three months' individual attention for about one-half hour daily)

"Learning has presented a difficulty for Sam because of his complete confusion regarding direction; that is, the left-to-right movement in reading the printed page, and in writing words on a line. In the beginning, when looking at a row of pictures, he named them from either left or right, or from the middle; and when attempting to write a short sentence in manuscript, he placed the words of the sentence anywhere on the paper, with no idea of sequence whatsoever. This happened even after he had been carefully instructed as to their sequential order.

"Consequently, it seemed necessary to establish the proper directional pathway, visually and kinesthetically, before expecting him to continue with any kind of formal classwork. Therefore, the type of individual instruction given him has been an attempt to accomplish this purpose.

"The individual procedures used have been as follows:

1. <u>Training in left-to-right direction.</u> Examples:

   a. "Sam observed me arrange, left to right, a row of three or more toy animals. Then I scattered them and asked him to place them as I had.[1] (At first he could not do this at all.) The same process was repeated, using not toy animals but three or more individual pictures of animals: dog, cat, rabbit, etc.

   "As an auditory aid, he was encouraged to name aloud the toy animals, and those in the pictures as he placed them. This helped his recall during the process of reassembling them in the original order.

   b. "Sam did orally the exercises in <u>The Red Book</u>.[2] This is a workbook containing pictures only. Most of the exercises are arranged in rows, four to eight pictures to a row, and about six rows to the page. For Sam, in addition to the exercises, the value of the book was that he could slide his finger along each row from left to right and cover the entire page with proper left-to-right movements.

---

1. See Anna Gillingham and Bessie W. Stillman, <u>Remedial Training for Children with Specific Disability in Reading, Spelling and Penmanship, Part One, The Problem</u>. Fourth edition, 1946, p. 35. Distributed by Anna Gillingham, 25 Parkview Ave., Bronxville 8, N.Y.
2. Thelma Gwinn Thurstone, <u>The Red Book</u>, Learning to Think Series, Science Research Associates, Chicago, Ill., 1949. (Latest revision is 1959.)

c. "Sam drew a series of lines from left to right, in ladder formation, on the blackboard; then followed the lines with his finger. This activity provided further kinesthetic aid.

"At all times in drills b and c his attention was called to the direction in which his fingers and eyes were traveling. Then he was shown how the same procedure is followed in reading the printed page. Also, a small strip of adhesive tape was pasted on his left wrist each day to remind him that he was to start from the left. (He knows now when he goes the wrong way—but regression still occurs occasionally.)

"A glance back over a, b, and c will show that care was taken to provide repeated drill in auditory, visual, and kinesthetic experiences before confronting Sam with a return to reading and writing.

2. Training in cursive writing.

"In teaching cursive writing, the methods of Grace Fernald were followed. On the chalkboard there was placed in large cursive writing a sentence dictated by Sam and usually descriptive of a picture he had drawn. Then he followed with his finger one of the words on the chalkboard until he knew it and could reproduce it without a copy. As he traced or wrote, he was encouraged to say the sounds of each syllable as he wrote that syllable. (Synchronization is the point of this combined saying-writing procedure.) The process was repeated for other words in the sentence.

"At this time he can write short sentences by employing this method. He seems to be right-handed and has always chosen to use this hand when writing.

"It is my belief that it is very much wiser for him to continue large cursive handwriting instead of manuscript. My reasons are as follows:

a. "The flow of cursive writing from left to right has been helpful

70

in establishing direction for Sam.

b. "He still reverses and confuses 'b,' 'd,' 'p,' 'q,' and 'f' in manuscript.

c. "He has had great success with the cursive. His manuscript was always untidy and erratic, but he does cursive writing easily and neatly after tracing. To illustrate how delighted he was with his success, one day when I came to him he surprised me with ten words he had written. He rushed up and pointed to the chalkboard. 'Look what I done! Look what I done!' It had taken time for him to develop this much independence of action.

3. <u>Training in phonics.</u>

"After Sam had succeeded with cursive writing and had gained some confidence in himself, a more specific plan of word attack was introduced by slow degrees. Adaptations of the word-building method stressing visual, auditory, and kinesthetic relationships for each phonogram presented were begun, and he was managing the program without difficulty."[3]

---

3. To switch gradually into another method may seem like heresy to some. However, this is an example of a case in which it did seem wise, and it was working for Sam when he left our school. His self-esteem had been helped dramatically by the ease with which he had learned to write; his health had improved; he was prepared physically and psychologically to begin an alphabetic type of approach to the language. It was hoped that he would not be expected to compete in a large class and that arrangements would be made for him to continue with the kind of individual, remedial help that would give him both psychological and neurophysiological support in achieving use of the language.

Thus, for reasons of the total make-up—physical, psychological, temperamental—we sometimes have to experiment with method or combinations of methods that will help to bring both comfort and competence to the child.

As Katrina de Hirsch says: "Since every individual recognizes printed symbols in different ways, different methods may have to be used with different individuals. The child who has trouble correlating visual images with meaning because his visual recall is poor has to capitalize on his auditory competence. . . . The youngster with a spelling difficulty needs phonics more than others do. . . .

"For some children auditory and visual stimuli need to be reinforced by kinesthetic ones." Katrina de Hirsch, "Specific Dyslexia or Strephosymbolia," <u>Folia Phoniatrica</u>, Vol. 4, No. 4 (1952), p. 240 (published by S. Karger, Basel/ New York).

Name: Scott V.   (typical American boy—lively, with many interests)

Age: 12 years

Grade: Low 7

Attendance: 8 months

Personal Note

Scott's family consisted of the parents and four boys, all of whom thoroughly enjoyed one another.

Reason for Presentation

The notation on Scott has been included to show that there are values in having different age levels in a group, at least for a part of the school day.   Interaction can produce good results scholastically, socially, and psychologically.

Excerpts from School Progress Report (which was written at the end of eight months' time)

"Scott is a very competent and promising student, with intellectual interests.   He has been the oldest one in a varied age group here, and none of the others has been as advanced as he.

"His strong interests have been the world news in the newspaper, Current Events, and the music--and he has done excellent work in both. In fact, he has pursued social studies material with the greatest zest. For example, in delving for information on South America and on the functioning of the United Nations, he made two very creditable notebooks containing drawings, pictures, and appropriate written comment.   And in music he has shown cultivated tastes.   He loves the best in musical composition, and since percussion instruments are all that have been available to him here, he has enjoyed tapping out favorite themes on the tone bells.   This interest and pleasure in music were responsible also for stimulating the entire group of boys (fifteen in number) to work out a fine orchestration with percussion instruments for the Finale of Beethoven's Fifth Symphony.

"As for language arts, spelling is easy for Scott and has been done very satisfactorily.   Written composition has been fairly good, but at times carelessly done. He has fine comprehension of what he reads, although it has not been easy to foster much interest in literature.

"His ability in arithmetic is good. However, we had to review fundamental processes while covering work in decimals, percentage, denominate numbers, areas, volume, and graphs. A few weeks' concentrated coaching in arithmetic would be very helpful in making him secure at grade level.

"It is important to say in this report that Scott has been a very fine influence in our ward schoolroom. He has been wonderful about teaching the little boys, and he has been responsible and reliable in every way."

Follow-up

A check eight years later showed that Scott was a junior in college, chosen for Who's Who in American Colleges and Universities, and president of a foreign-language honor society.

Name: Sally M. (indifferent, resentful child)

Age: 9 years, 5 months

Grade: High 4

Attendance: 3 months

Personal Note

Accurate information was not known. The father seemed to be away often; the mother worked at night; frequent moves seemed to be a constant factor.

Reason for Presentation

The notation on Sally has been included to show how the possible effects of frequent moves and almost total lack of any previous school preparation were handled.

Observation and Comment on Sally:

A Revised Stanford-Binet test score of 96 indicated that learning should proceed satisfactorily for this child. In trying to help her, getting her to face the problem of building a foundation for her work was a long process. When the lacks in preparation are so many, it has been my experience that, in making a start, the focusing of major concentration on <u>one</u> <u>phase</u> of endeavor is often helpful. In this case, I was guided by Sally's own interest, which seemed to be learning how to do some arithmetic.

<u>Excerpts from School Progress Report</u> (which was written at the end of three months' time)

"According to a previous school report, Sally has had unfortunate home conditions and a school history indicating many interruptions and changes. It may be because of these circumstances that she has shown such complete lacks in all of the essential basic skills. Consequently, the plan has been to help her build some confidence and skill by concentrating on one thing at a time. For a beginning, she has been using pennies as objects to gain the concepts of simple counting and of addition and subtraction processes. It has been rather amazing to watch her work at this. She concentrates for an hour or more, moving the pennies as she works out her answers. By now, perhaps, she has had enough experience to begin on higher addition and simple multiplication processes, but it is my opinion that she will need objects to count for some time yet. If she is not pushed too quickly into processes for which she is not ready, she should be able to hold her gains, because she has achieved beginning success in arithmetic.

"It has been my purpose to encourage her reading efforts gradually. By now, it is easier to introduce more regular reading habits. The other day she read for a half-hour period—her longest span. At present the books chosen should be of a very easy vocabulary level with greater interest content—even primer level to gain fluency. It has seemed to help if I read along with her. She needs much encouragement, and it is only lately that she would talk to me soberly about her school difficulties. She said she thought she was stupid.

"Sally loves to make designs and she enjoys music and rhythm activities. She came here listed as a high-fourth-grader, but she will continue to need basic foundation built in all her work."

Name: Sheila G. (unhappy child at time of enrollment)

Age: 10 years, 6 months

Grade: Low 5

Attendance: 3 months

Personal Note

Four members of Sheila's family were chronically ill. Since the mother worked, this situation made it difficult for her to visit Sheila more than once every two weeks.

Reason for Presentation

The notation on Sheila has been included to show that separation from home and living in an institution are very difficult adjustments for some children. During her first weeks with us, this highly intelligent child was extremely resistant to her plight and her environment.

Since dislike of arithmetic was her school problem, the notation has been included also, to make an additional point—which is that time spent by the teacher in settling down and working through a learning process difficulty right then, when the pupil reaction is stormy, can be a very important gain for some pupils.

Observation and Comment on Sheila

In Sheila's case the arithmetic bugbear was multiplication. Shortly after her arrival, she became angered and frustrated by the multiplication section in a page of test problems. She cried. She raged that she never would "be able to do problems like these" and she "hated this place anyway!" By sitting down beside her, beginning step by step to do the problems myself—by cajoling this irate student into contributing a little help, and gradually more help, toward solution, it was possible to convince her that she could manage to conquer the troublesome process.

Excerpts from School Progress Report (which was written at the end of three months' time)

"During her three months in the ward classroom, Sheila has proven to be a most interesting pupil. She has some mature intellectual interests and shows unusual understanding and perception for reading and social studies. Written expression has shown competence, too.

"While in the ward, perhaps the most significant gain made has been a great change in attitude. She seems gradually to have come to accept her stay in this institution, and has mastered the arithmetic which originally upset her so much. Security and successful experiences in this field are now established.

"Gradually, too, Sheila has become a cooperative member of the group and has entered willingly into activities which would help the younger children.

"She enjoys working with her hands. In particular, she loves to sew and does this kind of handwork easily and neatly.

"It is my opinion that Sheila should have the maximum benefits that a liberal-arts education has to offer."

Follow-up

A visit with Sheila ten years later revealed that she was a freshman in college—an enthusiastic student, doing well, and holding a job, too.

The Teacher and the Diversity

Following convalescence, it perhaps could be expected that some problems—physical ones, at least, and maybe certain school troubles—would show improvement. Obviously, though, the remainder of any difficulties requiring further attention would be inherited once again by the classroom teacher. The point to be re-emphasized is that among the children in every classroom there is a spread of diverse problems.

Take, for example, the daily newspaper accounts of families in complex difficulties. The children in these unhappy situations are in the classroom. In a democracy the school tries not to abandon them. Although the ordinary classroom is not the place for the maladjusted child (the one whose "emotional or psychological disorder" is "extreme and prolonged"),[4] the school does have an obligation to those whose

---

4. Charles L. C. Burns, M.R.C.S., L.R.C.P., D.P.M., F.B.Ps.S., Maladjusted Children, Hollis & Carter, Ltd., London, 1955, p. 1.

difficulties are not serious enough to disqualify them for learning and for usual classroom activities. How can they be helped to find some satisfactions through the school program? How can they be helped to behave so that everyone in the group is free to learn? These are the realities for the teacher.

There is an acute need for cooperating community facilities to offer care for family problems, including those of mental health. With such assistance many more children could be helped to survive a period of unfortunate personal distress—thereby increasing their chances of becoming useful, contributing citizens, rather than disorganized personalities.

Meanwhile, however, children with problems are largely on the doorstep of the classroom teacher.

SAMPLE TOOL (A) PRIMARY GRADES

Individual Pupil Participation in Plan for Self-Evaluation

The idea of individual student participation in a plan for self-evaluation was tried with a small group of intermediate children. Through pupil check of daily accomplishment, improvement of work habits was fostered. No competition with others was involved. It was meant merely as an individual tabulation of accomplishment.

Directions: Each child made his own figure (e.g., an elf) and recorded for completion either checks or a brief notation in the blanks on a checking sheet. With reasonable daily accomplishment, he was allowed to choose a sticker to paste on the elf. His elf, or any other figure made by him, was placed in an envelope on the bulletin board or kept in his personal book stack--as he chose. His checking sheet was folded and attached to the elf.

This is a crude device, but some children seem to find it rewarding. (Adapted from ideas of Mrs. Marymary French, Remedial Teacher, Felton, California.)

SAMPLE TOOL (A)

W H A T   I   D I D

Jan. 10-14	Mon.	Tues.	Wed.	Thurs.	Fri.
Reading					
Social Studies					
Spelling Writing*					
Arithmetic					
Nature Science					
Art Music					
Free Choices	Clay	Puzzles	Stamps	Stamps	Puzzles

*Refers to creative writing, letters, or descriptions of personal paintings, drawings, construction work, experiences, etc.

SAMPLE TOOL (B)

CHART FOR CHECKING GAINS OR LOSSES IN CASES
OF SCHOOL FAILURES, IN CASES OF BEHAVIOR PROBLEMS,
AND FOR RECORDING FOLLOW-UP INFORMATION

NAME:

DATE OF REPORT:

ATTENDED FROM _____ TO _____

1. Children With Indications of School Failure

Results of Testing: Sept., Oct.	Results of Testing: May, June	Improved in which Subject Areas	Not Improved in which Subject Areas	Evidence		3. Follow-up Information
				Objective	Subjective	

2. Children Exhibiting Behavior Problems

Sept., Oct.	May, June	Improved How?	Not Improved How?	Evidence		Follow-up Information
				Objective	Subjective	

Note: The information to be recorded may be compiled on large individual cards.

79

CHAPTER IV

SOME USEFUL APPROACHES

Two Bold Experimenters

Besides achieving mastery of his particular field, the teacher, as he recognizes the depth and breadth of differences in children, learns to gain an ever widening knowledge of appropriate instructional materials and of basic principles underlying useful methods and their adaptations. He draws constantly on this growing store of information and is forever experimenting with ways in which to reach individual children, since it is through his individual and his group programs that much guidance is interlaced.

If he plans in an organized way for integrating the sensory-motor avenues, if he prepares to meet differences in imagery, if he explores possibilities for making associations more meaningful, he has an excellent basis for judging methods and devising adaptations of them. What he really does is to look beyond method into philosophy and learning principles that method will help him to employ. It seems useful to think in terms of "How can this method help me to provide reinforced learning experience?" And, "How can it help me to help the child 'construct' himself?"[1]

Two educators who have been bold in experimentation and who have achieved empirical results are Grace Fernald and Frank C. Laubach.

Grace M. Fernald

As a preliminary to discussing Fernald approaches, it is important to remember that a crucial thing to look for in method is provision for

---

1. Maria Montessori.

strengthening learning through kinesthetic experiences as well as through auditory and visual experiences. As an example, in the good social studies program it is common practice to accentuate kinesthetic learnings; it is a program of _doing,_ which also involves feelings, creates understandings, and builds associations and experience.

Similarly, operating on this same principle in the language arts, we recall that writing and speech become the _doing_ experiences in verbal learning. They are vital reinforcements for seeing and hearing. Synchronizing the use of the senses is exactly what happens when the techniques of Grace Fernald, or adaptations of them, are practiced.

In my opinion, it is unfortunate that the Fernald system is referred to as the kinesthetic system. Because of this tag, some assume that the techniques have limited use. Actually, Fernald's is a look, say, _and_ do method, providing opportunity for the expression of personal interests which in turn provide vital interest associations for remembrance.

In addition to personal experimentation in using and adapting Fernald techniques and combining them with other methods, evidence of their value from the reactions and testimonies of other teachers has been observed. It was my experience to visit a night extension class of elementary teachers who had learned how to adapt individual Fernald spelling techniques for classroom use.[2] They had taught children in large groups to synchronize speaking the syllables of the words softly, as they traced them. It was exciting to see their results—the class spelling-papers, the children's stories, the graphs of comparative performance—and to sense their general feeling of satisfaction and genuine enthusiasm for the benefits they had experienced.

Likewise worth noting is an article in the Grade Teacher which points to kinesthetic performance as a basic need in learning, and the application of Fernald procedures to the classroom is described.[3] Also

---

2. Instructed by Mrs. Marymary French, San Jose State College Extension, June, 1956.
3. Dorothea P. Shea, "The Case for the Kinesthetic Method," Grade Teacher, Vol. LXXIV, No. 2, Oct., 1956, pp. 60, 108, 110.

to be mentioned is an excerpt from the Foreword to Fernald's book by Lewis M. Terman. He states that the importance of Dr. Fernald's work "goes far beyond the treatment of extreme non-readers. For every child showing [extreme] disability there are hundreds with partial disability. [The] data presented . . . show that the method is also highly effective in raising the level of spelling and composition."[4]

Aside from the values of the prescribed Fernald techniques,[5] there is another extraordinarily important value in this repertoire. It concerns the diverse uses and adaptations to which individual verbal expression can be put, and provides composition experience and satisfaction for pupils who are achieving adequately, or better, as well as for those who are managing inadequately. I refer to the individual booklets that each child can make.[6]

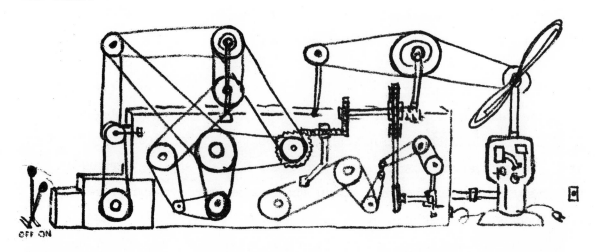

A drawing made for fun. Problem: "Why doesn't this machine work?" Answer: "Because it isn't plugged in!"
(Seventh grade boy.)

Into these booklets, the pupil can gradually put a variety of choices which may consist of his own drawings, magazine pictures, freehand maps, designs, plans for inventions, etc.

---

4. From Remedial Techniques in Basic School Subjects, by Grace M. Fernald, p. ix. Copyright, 1943. McGraw-Hill Book Co., New York, N.Y. Used by permission.
5. Ibid., pp. 35-55.
6. To describe one sample type, the books can be constructed very easily by using paper fasteners (rather than staples) to hold about ten sheets of newscut, preferably colored. The cover and back piece can be merely bright-colored construction paper—18 by 24 in. is a good size.

I Made the State Capitol. The State Capitol is where they Make laws.

Example of cursive writing—first grade.
(Boy, age 6.)

The Old Ford

    An old woman was riding in her old
Ford. She dropped an old fork on the
floor of the old Ford. It fell down a
hole in the old Ford. That is how holes
were first invented.

The Old Ford

Anold woman was riding in her old Ford. She dropped an old fork on the floor of the old Ford. It fell down a hole in the old Ford. That is how holes were first invented.
                    arnold

This is written work done by the Fernald tracing technique. (See p. 70.) Usually, the sheet with the pupil's handwriting is folded so that he does not see it as he reads the typed copy. If he needs to refresh his memory on individual words that he has not succeeded completely in associating with the typed form, he may look again at the handwritten copy. (Third grade boy, age 8.)

The Land of Teapots
Teapot Land is where
the little teapots live, and little
people live in them

(Third grade girl.)

Opposite his picture will be his own expression concerning it in typed form or in handwriting, or in both. Occasionally, he may wish to insert such things as extra drawings or paintings with no writing attached. (This is the reason paper fasteners are better than staples.)

To one mixed group of fifteen pupils, grades four to six, from whom it was difficult to obtain written work, a large stack of mounted pictures was offered. These pictures had a most amazing effect! Each child chose what he wanted to put into his book. One girl who loved horses chose pictures of horses, and within a few days had used encyclopedias for reference and had written a paragraph description for each horse chosen. One boy, customarily silent and unresponsive, also chose a picture of horses; he wrote a long story about stolen horses. Another boy chose forest and mountain scenery and wrote about his camping trips. He had been so quiet previously that it was not known what interest could vitalize him!

So the teacher learns, too, about her pupils—not only what their written language skills are, or are not, but something of what each one is thinking.

For the adequately prepared pupil, the book serves to hold the written record of some of his interests in organized form. It serves, too, as stimulation for written work, and is usually a source of pride to its owner.

84

For the inadequately prepared and discouraged pupil, the individual booklets can bring new hope. When such a child can be helped to make a fresh start with reading and spelling that come from his own experience, he feels encouraged. Seeing his own stories, his descriptions, or his plans typed and attached to the pages opposite his drawings (or other choices) brings him new self-respect. In fact, the effect on him can be wonderful. This is his material. He can read it. Confidence begins to grow. This one beginning procedure offers therapeutic aid for feelings of terrible inadequacy and an incentive for effort to practice and learn.[7]

One last comment on the individual booklets, whether for the fast or slow—it is helpful if everyone in the class has one. This is important to children. Usually, no one wants to be all alone in an activity of this sort, or to be without a booklet if the others have them.

I agree with Dorothea P. Shea that: "Kinesthetic learning is not the panacea for all learning difficulties, but its full implications have not been studied because such learning has not been thoroughly investigated for method, technique and application. Undoubtedly the greatest handicap to such study has been the belief that kinesthetic learning is a thing apart and cannot exist side by side with the academic, but once this is dissipated, kinesthetic learning bids fair to come into its own in a happy and united relationship with all learning forms."[8]

It is indeed true that for ordinary classroom application, much experimentation in the area of kinesthetic learning remains to be tried. We can learn from Montessori, Fernald, and Gillingham, who have so ably demonstrated its values.

---

7. It is my experience that it is helpful to permit the discouraged child to dictate his first efforts and to receive these back in typed form by the next day, at least (Fernald). Following this beginning step, the various "stages" of procedure recommended by Fernald may be used outright or adapted to fit the needs of the user. By being helped to practice these techniques, a pupil can gain confidence and the ability to do the writing for his own stories. As he gains in skill and security he is able to face books once again. (Secretarial assistance with typing is a great help, of course.)

8. Dorothea P. Shea, "The Case for the Kinesthetic Method," Grade Teacher, Vol. LXXIV, Number 2, Oct., 1956, p. 110. Reprinted from GRADE TEACHER magazine by permission of the publishers. Copyright 1956 by The Educational Publishing Corp.

Frank C. Laubach

It is easy to understand why Frank Laubach, a missionary, busy working at literacy for the world's millions, has been described as "one of the most influential private citizens alive."[9] He has demonstrated that reading and writing can be taught in minimum time to the most deprived and miserable persons in illiterate populations. Truly, the underprivileged world has been given new hope with the Laubach program of "Each One Teach One."[10]

Appropriately enough, Dr. Laubach's programs have been extended to reach adult illiterates in the United States.[11] His methods for instruction of native languages have been adapted for teaching reading in English.

In examining his Reading Readiness Charts and Stories[12] for English, which can be used with young children, it will be seen that a most ingenious technique for building associative memory for initial consonant and vowel sounds is presented. A picture is created to establish an association for each letter. This picture is drawn to correspond with the general shape of the letter. For example, the picture for the consonant "d" is made in the shape of a round plate with a knife placed directly beside it (to the right). Imposed on a second picture is the letter "d" followed by the word "dish." Since all of this sequence is placed in horizontal strip form on the chart, the various strips may be cut up for easy handling and drill. Such an associative device can be very helpful to children with a poor visual memory span for letters and words. One pupil who was delighted with these pictures wished to make up his own sentences for each picture, so the strips were attached to larger papers

---

9. Robert Rice, "The Thousand Silver Threads," The New Yorker, Vol. XXVII, No. 53, Feb. 16, 1952, p.38.
10. Margaret Lee Runbeck, "Each One Teach One," Woman's Day, Dec., 1954, pp. 33, 70-73.
11. David C. Stewart, "Reading, Writing, and Television," Harper's, Vol.218, No. 1309, June, 1959, pp. 58-59. Note: There have been numerous articles in magazines about Dr. Laubach within the last few years. Articles showing pictures of the charts appeared in Life, Vol. 42, No. 4, Jan. 28, 1957, p. 47, and Newsweek, Vol. LII, No. 1, July 7, 1958, p. 50.
12. Frank C. Laubach, Reading Readiness Charts and Stories, Koinonia Foundation Press, Pikesville Box 5744, Baltimore 8, Md. Copyright 1955 by Frank C. Laubach.

on which he could write, and on which his typed sentences could be pasted.

One aspect, only, of Dr. Laubach's system has been discussed here. It is a fine example of how pictures and form (or shape) are combined to help establish association—a built-in technique.[13]

It should not go unmentioned that in his literacy program there is the greatest consideration for the feelings of the pupil. The learner is treated with respect and confidence, and with affection, too. Edgar A. Doll expressed the same regard for the individual when he said that "one of the first principles of successful education is the affection that goes with it."[14]

Examples of Written Expression

The following are a few examples of ways in which children expressed themselves in writing in individual, small group, and large group efforts.

13.

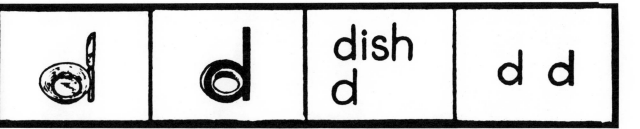

(Copy of material published in Reading Readiness Charts and Stories, by Frank C. Laubach.)

In connection with what may make a meaningful association, individuality again enters the picture. An intelligent child of eight years could not remember her telephone number. Nothing worked. Finally, her mother used music. She sang the numbers to a little tune, and then they stuck!

14. Edgar A. Doll, Director of Special Education, Bellingham, Wash. Lecture at Frederic Burk School, San Francisco, Calif., July 28, 1951.

Example of individual expression
(Fifth grade girl, age 8 1/2.)

88

- Chapter I -

THE LOST RING

Mrs. Little lost her ring in the bathtub pipe.

She asked Stuart to please get her ring. Stuart got down in the pipe and he found the ring. After Stuart came out of the pipe his mother thanked him.

(Boy, age 8.)

Example of a chapter from the children's version of Stuart Little, by E.B. White

A group of boys loved this book. They divided up the main incidents of the story, each choosing a particular part to write about and to illustrate. In some instances several boys composed together. All written work was typed and compiled so that each boy had his own copy of the complete story. The size of the big illustrated book was 18" by 24".

(Grades 1-5.)

Greta¹ Comes

After while, Captain Cook gets sick. He is lonesome. So a man sends another penguin to Mr. Popper. Her name is Greta. She lays ten eggs!

(Third grade boy, age 8.)

Mr. Popper's Penguins, by Atwater, was equally successful in stimulating written expression.

(Grades 3-5.)

90

① How to Make Puppets

The first step in puppet making is to model your puppet with clay.

The second step is to glue several strips of paper on the clay puppet. If you don't put several strips of paper on the puppet, when you cut it in half the puppet will break.

② The third step is to let the puppet dry for over an hour.

The fourth step is to cut the puppet in half. This is done so you can take the clay out of the puppet.

The fifth step is to take the clay out of the puppet.

The sixth step is to glue the two parts

③ of the puppet together.

The seventh step is to think of the clothes that you want for your puppet.

The eighth step is to sew the clothes together.

The ninth step is to put the clothes on the puppet.

The last step is

to think up your show and put the show on the stage!

D. J. and B. W.

Example of a written record of a particular process

Two boys worked jointly to think through these steps in the puppet-making process and to put them in writing.

(Fifth grade, ages 10 years.)

UNITED NATIONS WEEK

This is United Nations week. This morning two nurses came in to school to tell us about their countries.

Miss R__ showed us on the globe how far it is from Germany to California. She showed us pictures of Germany, and she told us about some of the things she did when she was a little girl. We heard about the celebration of Christmas and Fast time. Miss R__ told us that the first Christmas trees were trimmed in Germany. Real candles were used to decorate them.

The **outdoor** clocks in Germany are big and tall. This is because they are old. People didn't have many clocks in their houses and they had to look up to see what time it was.

In one big clock the twelve apostles come out of a box behind the clock when it is twelve o'clock.

Girls and boys in Germany like to hike in the woods. The forests are very pretty.

Miss N__ told us about Holland. The people eat eels there. They cook them in big kettles out in the street.

Holland is below sea level. They build dikes in their country to keep the water away from their villages and farms.

The Dutch people milk the cows by hand. In the United States we use machines to milk cows on the big farms.

People in Holland built walls around some of their towns. This was centuries ago.

Miss N__ gave us a piece of Dutch chocolate. We liked the chocolate. We wish we had more! It was so delicious!

Paul and Joe came in and played a Chinese instrument for us. It belonged to the String Family. It was one hundred years old. Some of the songs they played for us were about the banana tree and rain, and the peacock and the butterfly.

They wrote Ruby Jean and Brenda in Chinese. They played Chinese records, too.

(Girls' group, grades 3-5.)

HALLOWE'EN NIGHT

'Twas on Hallowe'en night
There was a moon so full.

And the grave yard was
   still
As it began to fill

With a scary spook and
   goblin
And an old witch
   a-hobblin'.

She had creaky bones and
   straggly hair
And she went flying
   around
In a rocking chair!

(Girls' group, grades 3-8.)

Examples of group composition

In these examples the teacher wrote the children's dictation at the chalkboard. From their desks, they wrote with her. Together, as the dictation proceeded, they analyzed, sounded out, and spelled the words that were important for study. Sentence building and paragraph study were included, too.

Each child had his own handwritten copy and, eventually, a typed copy for his composition book.

92

(Third grade boy, age 8.)

(Fourth grade boy, age 8.)

On the Hill

Julio's picture looks like a house running up a hill. As you know, artists do not make the whole street. And across the street is a ferry building.

Julio's picture is a very nice picture.

A.J.

Example of one child's written impressions of a classmate's picture

Application for the Arts

Consider next the arts--indispensable sources of expressive, creative, and integrative experience.[15]

In keeping with the major theme of this book, planning for the inter-related use of the sensory-motor pathways is introduced again, this time into the teaching of music. Records ranging from simple rhythms to symphonies, rhythm instruments, and art media such as chalks, crayons, and finger paints are the necessary props. The manner in which the ideas are worked out is planned to help children achieve "movement, feeling, and thought."[16]

In seeking to accomplish the objective of inducing "movement, feeling, and thought," three activities involving music and other art experience are presented. These activities are separate, but there is unity and relationship among them. They are: (1) free motion to music, using

---

15. "As long as emotional growth is separated from intellectual growth, the child will develop inconsistently." Reprinted with the permission of the publisher from Creative and Mental Growth, by Viktor Lowenfeld, p.43. Copyright 1957 by The Macmillan Company, New York, N.Y.

16. "We apprehend the world through three chief functions: movement, feeling and thought. However, an individual does not begin life with all three actively employed. Usually one or two are used; the third is more or less asleep in the unconscious. Buried within the neglected capability may be the key to the development of a particular individual. The teacher's role is to find ways of activating the unused function.

"An integrated individual is one who makes a well-balanced use of each of these three forms of activity. Art has three precepts which must be followed if one is to obtain its fullest expression. There is a correspondence between these functions of the human being and the underlying principles of art. The function of movement is related to the principle of rhythm; feeling, to dynamics and harmony; and thought, to balance. Since the principles of art correspond to human functions, one may therefore gradually integrate functions through the practice of art. By this fortunate relation, the teaching of art can be a valuable method for the growth and integration of the individual." Florence Cane, The Artist in Each of Us, Pantheon Books, New York, N.Y., 1951, p. 34.

art media; (2) music analysis, using records and percussion instruments in an involved type of rhythm band experience;[17] and (3) design to music, using art media and design principles while applying knowledge of music analysis. Putting the plan in outline form indicates the direction of the objective. It is as follows:

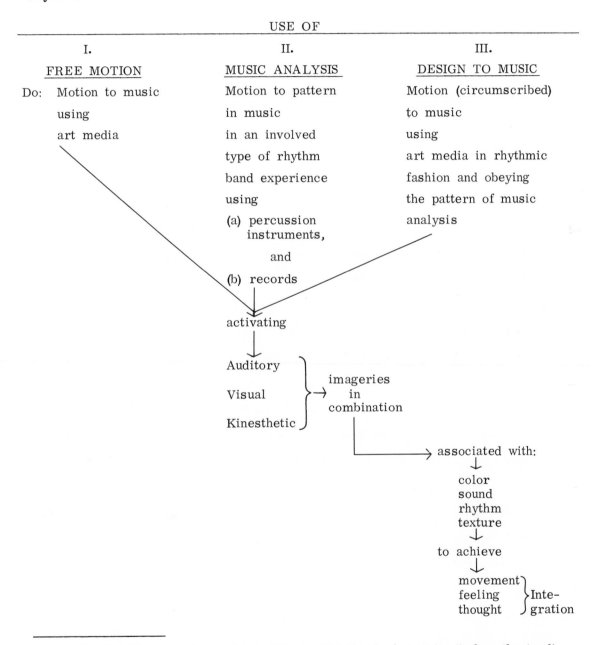

USE OF

I.	II.	III.
FREE MOTION	MUSIC ANALYSIS	DESIGN TO MUSIC

Do: Motion to music using art media

Motion to pattern in music in an involved type of rhythm band experience using
(a) percussion instruments, and
(b) records

Motion (circumscribed) to music using art media in rhythmic fashion and obeying the pattern of music analysis

activating

Auditory
Visual
Kinesthetic

imageries in combination

associated with:
color
sound
rhythm
texture
to achieve
movement
feeling
thought
Integration

17. Teaching music analysis through this kind of activity "takes the traditional rhythm band off the play shelf"* and utilizes it for more serious music education and experience. If analysis is taught in this way, such activities are suitable for intermediate children as well as primary. *Dorothy Ketman (formerly Supervisor of Music, Palo Alto School System, Palo Alto, Calif.).

The following directions are mainly for teachers who may be interested in making application of the neurophysiological approach to music, combining it in some instances with various art experiences.

More specifically, now, what music, what art media can be used to carry out the plan?

Directions would be as follows for:

I. Free Motion

Step A. Taking a moderately long piece of music—the "Polka" from The Bartered Bride, for example—play the music and have the children move their fingers over the paper (size 1 1/2 by 2 ft., at least) with rhythmic free arm and shoulder motions. After they have achieved some feeling for freedom of movement, go through the same motions to the music using soft crayons (Sketcho). One value of a long music selection is that the sweep and motion of the music have a chance to seep into the listeners, helping to produce relaxation and freedom of motion. Other good selections for this activity are "The Blue Danube," and "Ballabili" from Aida. (See Plates I and II.)

Step B. Next, change the art medium to finger paints. Before spreading the paint substance, repeat the idea of moving the finger tips over the paper (being sure arm and shoulder motions are easy and relaxed); then finger paint to works such as Mozart's "Jupiter" Symphony (No. 41 in C),[18] Beethoven's Fifth Symphony,[19] and Grieg's Piano Concerto in A Minor.[20]

In one experiment, a sheet of paper 2 1/2 by 4 feet in size provided a child with a fine opportunity for individual freedom of motion. For another experiment in which collective action was attempted, seven children were placed standing at intervals along the sides of a long table. One extensive piece of white butcher's paper was used, and the aesthetic

18. Suggest part of the Third Movement.
19. Suggest part of the Finale.
20. Suggest part of the First Movement.

experience of listening and moving to Beethoven's "Emperor" Concerto (last movement) yielded a highly spectacular and colorful twelve-foot mural in finger paint.[21] (See Plates III and IV.)

II. Music Analysis

Music analysis helps to make particular music selections part of oneself. It involves a uniting of both feeling and thought. It means learning to listen to a musical composition with gradually developing ability to determine the sequence of tune patterns (or motifs) making up the whole. For example, in listening to the "March" from the Nutcracker Suite[22] the same tune is distinguished four times:

> Tune 1
>
> Tune 1
>
> Tune 1
>
> Tune 1

More complex are tune patterns from such music as "Jalousie,"[23] "March of the Siamese Children" from The King and I, or "March of the Toys" from Babes in Toyland. Of course, the teacher must work out the analysis of any music in advance of class time; he must know the tune pattern perfectly. Communicating the idea of tune sequence, however, is not at all difficult if he employs visual reinforcement at the chalkboard while the children go through motions— first without instruments, and then with instruments as they establish mental concept and memory for following the tune patterns.

It is wise to commence in a simple way. Consequently, when introducing the idea of listening for tune sequences, begin with a short selection which illustrates one tune only. For instance, before playing the "March" from the Nutcracker Suite, tell the children they are about to hear a tune that repeats itself four times. "A tune is

---

21. Preceding the music, liquid starch was poured on the paper. Then the tempera powder paint was sprinkled on the starch. Each child painted his own area, blending it in with his neighbor's.

22. Rhythmic Activities, RCA Victor, Basic Rhythms Program, Vol. II.

23. Pan-American (Pan 032A) (written by J. Gade, played by Noel de Selva).

like a story, maybe short, maybe long. We will hear this particular story four times, one right after the other."

At this point, directions are as follows:

Step A. (1) Begin the "March" and as it plays, chalk down marks at the the board something like this:

Tune 1 - /////////////////////////////////
Tune 1 - /////////////////////////////////
Tune 1 - /////////////////////////////////
Tune 1 - /////////////////////////////////

(2) Play the same music again. Teacher and children do the following:

Teacher (at chalkboard)	Children (without instruments)
(a) Move fingers in rhythm along the marks from left to right. Accentuate the end of each tune by smacking the board with the fist.	(a) Clap hands together - Tune 1 Clap hands on thighs - Tune 1 Clap hands on shoulders - Tune 1 Clap fist on fist - Tune 1 Each time as the tune begins call out: "First!" "Second!" "Third!" "Fourth!"
(b) Play record again. Give no cue at end of tune. Do children remember to change the form of clapping activity, signifying awareness each time that the end of the tune has been reached?	(b) Go through the same motions. Watch teacher move her fingers along the marks on the chalkboard.

Step B. (1) Change music. Use "Broom Dance"[24] next. The piece has a short introduction, and this part of the music is easy to explain: "It introduces a tune just as you would introduce a person."

The pattern is:

Introduction - / / /

Tune 1 - /////////////////////////////

---

24. "Broom Dance," RCA Victor, #20448-B.

98

Tune 1 - /////////////////////////////////////

Tune 1 - /////////////////////////////////////

Repeat (all)

(A slight variation which has a rolling sound is noted the second and third time the tune is played.)

(2) Children watch and clap in time while the teacher chalks down the marks to the music.[25]

(3) Next, the children use three varieties of instruments such as sticks, maracas, and tambourines. (The teacher moves the fingers of one hand along the marks on the chalkboard, at the same time using the other hand to accentuate the beats.)

The first time Tune 1 plays, one group taps the sticks; the second time Tune 1 plays, another group comes in with the maracas (sticks quiet); and the third time Tune 1 plays, the last group uses the tambourines (all other instruments quiet).

Attention to listening while simultaneously watching the teacher's activity at the chalkboard helps to reinforce the memory of each group to stop playing at the end of its particular Tune 1.

It will be noted that the purpose of the instruments at this time is not for orchestration, but for tune identification.

Step C. (1) Use "Toreador Song" to illustrate bridges (or interludes) in music. "What does a bridge do?" "Listen for the main tune." "How many times can you hear it?" "How many bridges are there?" "Are they all the same?"

---

25. Another way to establish concept and memory for tune patterns is to have the children chalk out the pattern at the same time the teacher is doing this at the chalkboard. For example, using soft chalks or Sketcho on large paper, or soft chalks on desk-size blackboards, the process of jotting down (in rhythm to the music) a different cue marking for each tune helps to imprint the pattern of the music into the consciousness of the children. The use of a different colored chalk for each tune is also a contributing associative aid.

In my experience, soft chalks or Sketcho are better media than wax crayons. The latter seem to be too hard a medium for purposes of fast, easy execution of movement.

The tune sequence in this short selection is:

Tune 1 -

Bridge -

Tune 1 -

Bridge -

Tune 1 -

Bridge -

Tune 1 -

(2) Note that there are four Tune 1's once again. However, the music is fast and Bridges 1 and 3 are different from Bridge 2. These kinds of incidentals need attention.

(3) Divide class into four groups this time. Each group has its own Tune 1 and each claps it out as the teacher moves her fingers across the markings on the board. Motions for bridges must be different.

(4) Again practice, this time with instruments, each group having different instruments.[26]

Step D. Following this type of practice, progression moves into short selections with two tunes, the pattern being 1-2-1-2-1-2, for example, or 1-1-2-1-1.[27]

Step E. (1) When introducing orchestration, the teacher may impose the first experience of this sort. That is to say, impose orchestration of a short piece so that not much time is consumed. In this way, the children can see how certain instruments play different tunes (or parts of tunes); and they become aware that each person must be prepared to play at the right moment. After this imposed experience, they can move quickly into working out their own orchestrations. For

---

26. Since record companies seem to change arrangements, it is not possible to list arrangements guaranteed to be available indefinitely. Therefore, the analyses given should be thought of as guides for what the teacher may do himself. For example, the current arrangement for "Toreador Song" in Rhythmic Activities, RCA Victor, Basic Rhythms Program, Vol. IV, is Tune 1 played three times instead of four, and interspersed with two bridges instead of three.

27. Any selections having simple tune patterns from Rhythmic Activities albums or Listening Activities albums, RCA Victor, may be used.

example, impose the following for La Raspa":[28]

Tune 1 - Maracas, Drums, Wood Blocks
Tune 2 - Tambourines, Bells, Cymbals
Tune 1 - Repeat 1 above
Tune 2 - Repeat 2 above
Tune 1 -
Tune 2 -
Tune 1 -
Tune 2 -
Tune 1 -
Tune 2 -
Tune 1 and Ending - All play

(a) Clap hands in time to music (children). Tune 1
    Chalk down markings at chalkboard in time to music (teacher).

(b) Clap hands on thighs in time to music (children). Tune 2
    Chalk down markings at chalkboard in time to music (teacher).

(c) Explain and write on chalkboard (as above) that tambou-
    rines, drums, and maracas play Tune 1; that cymbals
    and triangles play Tune 2 (teacher).

(d) Practice; then have the children exchange instruments and
    repeat performance.

(2) Continue to point out difference and variety in pattern. Play
"Norwegian Dance."[29] Again, teacher chalks down marks
while children make different hand motions for Tune 1 and
Tune 2.

(3) Finally, analyze "Norwegian Dance" for what plays when and
where. Write the children's suggestions on the chalkboard—
like this, for example:

Tune 1 - Triangles, Tom-tom
Tune 1 - Bells, Xylophones
Tune 2 - All above; add Cymbals, Castanets, Maracas
Tune 1 - Triangles, Tom-tom
Tune 1 - Bells, Xylophones

Or, as another example, "Virginia Reels"[30] is a particularly
good choice. It is lively, the tunes are familiar, there is a
sequence of at least three or more tunes, and the children
are pleased to have the experience of managing a long, easy

---

28. "La Raspa" (Mexican Folk Dance), Imperial, #1084.
29. Rhythmic Activities, RCA Victor, Basic Rhythms Program, Vol. V.
30. "Virginia Reels," RCA Victor, #20447-B.

selection early in the music analysis process. (Concentration must be complete!) When the sequence is fairly well mastered, take up the tunes step by step for orchestration. What instruments fit this tune? One group worked out the following orchestration for "Virginia Reels":

Introduction - Cymbals
Tune 1 - Bells, Sand Blocks
Tune 1 - Triangles, Sand Blocks   "Miss McCloud's
Tune 1 - Tone Bell, Triangles, Sand Blocks,   Reel"
        Tom-tom
Tune 1 - Tone Bell, Triangles, Sand Blocks,
        Tom-tom
Tune 2 - Maracas, Tom-tom, Wood Block,
        Castanets, Xylophone   "Old Dan
                                                   Tucker"
Tune 2 - Same

Tune 3 - Cymbals, Wood Block, Xylophone
Tune 4 - Triangles, Bells, Tom-tom   "Pop Goes the
Tune 3 - Cymbals, Wood Block, Xylophone   Weasel"
Tune 4 - Triangles, Bells, Tom-tom

Note: "Pop Goes the Weasel" is divided into two tunes.

Repeat - in entirety.

As a suggested orchestration gradually unfolds, it is written out on the chalkboard in the above fashion.[31] Individual tunes are practiced and then combined with those tunes preceding, and those following, until the entire orchestration is put together. Here, again, as the class practices, the teacher uses one hand to point to the appropriate line on the chalkboard, moving her hand down through the tune sequence while she keeps time to the music with the other hand.

After several practice lessons, the children know the sequence of tune patterns and the orchestration. They no longer need the chalkboard memo. They still need practice for expression, rhythm, coordination of parts, and improved execution.

Comment:

To illustrate how analysis may be managed in the case of a more

---

31. Many children can manage more than one instrument and are able to change instruments at the designated times. In fact, they can become so expert with the analysis that they perform the change easily.

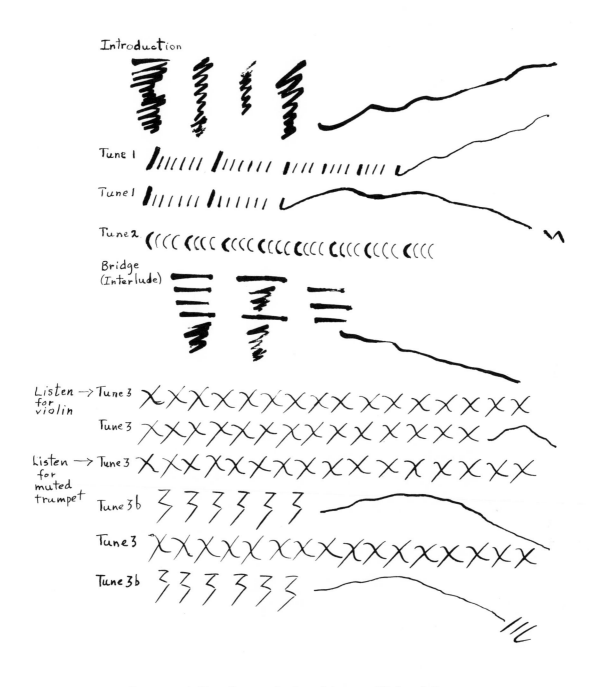

Representation for analysis of tunes, "Jalousie"

This is a visual device which may be used to aid in identifying the pattern of tunes. The chart should be large, at least 4 by 5 ft., and different colored chalks are used to denote the tune sequences. The teacher does not need to spend much time in making such a device. The main thing is to get across the idea of tune pattern.

complex piece of music—"Jalousie,"[32] for example—the pupils are exposed to a large chart on which each tune has been chalked in an individual way with its own particular color. While listening as the music plays, the children watch the teacher moving her hand along the tunes on the chart; they hum, and they use different motions for each tune, employing hands, feet, and bodies—or they may be divided into a number of groups corresponding to the number of tunes, and each group may use rhythm sticks to tap out the rhythm of the particular tune (Tune 1, Tune 2, etc.) assigned to it.

By developing music analysis in this way through attention to listening while watching visual cues, while humming, and while simultaneously using motion with hands or instruments, a full combination of sensory-motor activity, of imagery, and of association is in effect. Actually, in moving from simple tune patterns to more complex ones, it is amazing how quickly the complex ones can be attempted when the mental concept for analysis has been built.

III. Design to Music

When children have achieved relaxation and freedom of movement to music while simultaneously using an art medium, it is possible to work with smaller and more circumscribed motions. As preparation, one way to introduce the idea of moving to the exact beat of the music is to begin with music and song that suggests something known to the youngsters—something very definite. For example:

Step A. Using soft crayon (Sketcho), let the hands move, or dance, on the paper[33] to such songs as "The Little Marionettes" or "Funiculi, Funicula" ("The Little Railroad Train"). Moving their fingers in time to the music beats, the children sketch out in short strokes their ideas of little marionettes or the railroad train. "Trot, My Pony, Trot" and "There Was a Little Man Called Aiken Drum" are other suggestions.[34] (See Plates V, VI, VII, VIII.)

---

32. "Jalousie," Pan-American (Pan 032A).
33. Size—18 by 24 in. Or, using colored chalk on small desk-size blackboards is good, too.
34. Childcraft Mercury Records, No. 10, "Folk Songs of Other Lands." All four songs are on this record.

104

From SCHEHERAZADE-
The Vessel is Wrecked

MUSIC

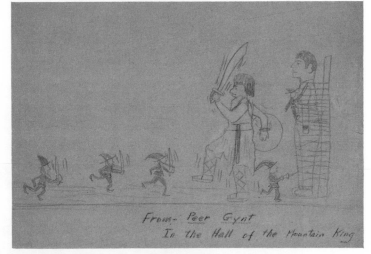

From- Peer Gynt
In the Hall of the Mountain King

FROM- PEER GYNT
In the Hall of the Mountain King

Plate I
Motion to The Blue Danube, by Strauss

Plate II
Motion to "Ballabili" from Aida, by Verdi

The pictures for all ten music plates were done by girls, ranging from third to eighth grades.

106

Plate III

Motion to "Jupiter" Symphony,
by Mozart (From Third Movement)

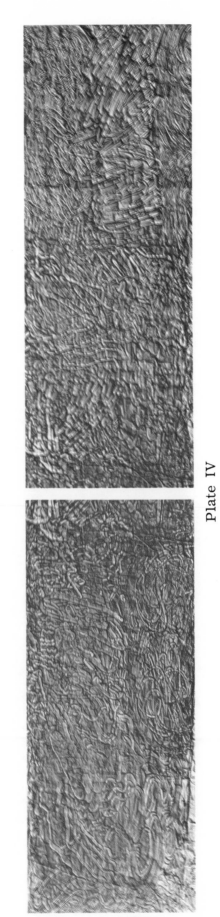

Plate IV

Motion to "Emperor" Concerto, by Beethoven (From Third Movement)

107

The Little Marionettes

See the dance they do,
O the little marionettes.
See the dance they do,
Three little turns and
    off they go!

Plate V

Plate VI

Plate VII

Funiculi, Funicula

Some think the world is made
    for fun and frolic,
And so do I!
    and so do I!
Some think it well
    to be all melancholic,
To pine and sigh,
    to pine and sigh.
But I, I love to spend
    my time in singing
Some joyous song,
    some joyous song;

To set the air
    with music bravely ringing
Is far from wrong!
    is far from wrong!

Chorus:

    Listen, listen!
        Music fills the air,
    Listen, listen!
        Joy is everywhere.
    Funiculi, funicula,
        funiculi, funicula!
    Joy is everywhere,
        funiculi, funicula.

Plate VIII

DESIGN TO MUSIC

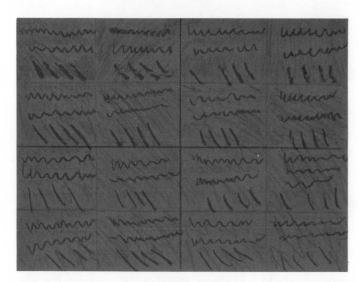

Plate IX

Motion to "Scherzo" from Symphony No. 3, Beethoven. (Tune pattern is 1-1-1-1 and each section represents one tune. This short selection was played four times.)

Plate X

Motion to Legend of the Bells, by Planquette. (Tune pattern is 1-1-2-2-1-1-2-2. Color was applied before playing music. Motion to music in tune sequence was accomplished in the alternating sections. Motion to Tune 1 was done in the blue sections and to Tune 2 in the purple sections.)

Step B. A next step is moving the chalks to a short music selection
without words. "Sweet and Low"[35] may be interpreted pictorially,
individually, by moving one stroke to a beat in rhythm with the
music.

Step C. In building upon the above (in A and B), and in expanding a plan
for stimulating "movement, feeling, and thought," it may be interesting to some teachers to know of the work of Laura Bassi,
Rome, Italy. This gifted teacher devised a method of primary
education known as Integral Rhythmics. A major objective was
to help children "learn and assimilate the fundamental elements
of music under a form truly adapted to the psychology of the
very young."[36] One part of this education concerned the making of a design in rhythm to music.

The paintings in Plate IX and Plate X (done by intermediate-level
children to the "Scherzo" from Beethoven's Symphony No. 3 and to Planquette's Legend of the Bells)[37] show a complex type of adaptation of
these ideas—that is, combining and synchronizing all-over design patterns
with music analysis in rhythmic motion to the music. It is obvious that
this kind of challenge will yield defeat only, unless the group is well
prepared and experienced in all-over design technique, in music analysis,
and in rhythmic expression. As may be inferred, however, the successful combination of rhythm, of music analysis, and of design to music may
bring achievement to a high level of "movement, feeling, and thought."

Mental Health in the Classroom

A last consideration among approaches deals with matters necessary
to everyone's good mental health. Here are four of these. They provide

35. Listening Activities, RCA Victor, Basic Rhythms Program, Vol. I.
36. From typed material obtained from Signora Emma Pampiglione Bassi,
Rome, 1950. In my opinion, the work of this school has made a unique contribution, and permission to visit it would be a privilege.
37. Music selections used for motion in these paintings may be found in
Listening Activities, RCA Victor, Basic Rhythms Program, Vol. I.

other useful guideposts for the teacher.[38]

(1) To make—which refers to the need for creating something and saying, "I did it!"

(2) To have—which means the need for having something of one's own, something that gives satisfaction and a feeling that "It's mine."

(3) To belong—which refers first to a family, and second, to a school (in the case of a child).

(4) To be—which means the awareness of one's own personality and a feeling of worth.

What are the ways which will help this child to be? To belong? To have? And to make?

A Final Thought

It seems suitable to close this chapter with the passage from Emerson which follows. As a description reflecting the deeper spirit of teaching, it likely has few rivals.

> . . . If he can communicate himself he can teach, but not by words. He teaches who gives, and he learns who receives. There is no teaching until the pupil is brought into the same state or principle in which you are; a transfusion takes place; he is you and you are he; then is a teaching, and by no unfriendly chance or bad company can he ever quite lose the benefit.[39]

38. Elise H. Martens (formerly of the United States Office of Education), lecture at Frederic Burk School, San Francisco, Calif., July 28, 1951. The order in which they were given by Elise Martens has been reversed, but otherwise they are reported as nearly verbatim as possible.

39. Ralph Waldo Emerson, "Spiritual Laws," in The Complete Essays and Other Writings of Ralph Waldo Emerson, edited by Brooks Atkinson, Random House, Inc., New York, N.Y., 1940, p. 201.

CHAPTER V

THE MONTESSORI MOVEMENT

And now Maria Montessori.[1]

Montessori was a "rare combination of a physician of wide experience, a psychologist and anthropologist of deserved reputation, and an educator . . . a woman of creative and inventive genius and of tireless enthusiasm, capable of devoting all her energies with intense concentration to the special problem she is seeking to solve" wrote Ellen Yale Stevens,[2] who early in this century traveled to Italy to study her methods.

Montessori was a dynamic spirit who had within herself the components necessary to an interdisciplinary approach in teaching. Combined with her comprehensive background and her vision of education was her Darwinian ability to integrate her knowledge. She took the investigations of biology, anthropology, psychology, and the sociological sciences, coordinated their interpenetrations, and applied them in formulating a system of education. In America she is worthy not only of rediscovery, but also of discovery.

I say rediscovery because we need to become reacquainted with her methods; her careful training sequences for young children could be profitably re-examined today. I say discovery because we never have

---

1. The year 1957 marked the fiftieth anniversary of the opening of the first Casa dei Bambini (The House of Children) in Rome by Dr. Maria Montessori. The Montessori Movement is not so well known in the United States as it is in Europe and other parts of the world; however, the International Montessori Society, founded originally in 1929, is presently active in many countries. During World War II, Hitler and Mussolini both imposed bans on official Montessori activities; consequently, Dr. Montessori left Italy and carried on her work in India. After the war she returned to Europe (1946).

2. Ellen Yale Stevens, A Guide to the Montessori Method, Frederick A. Stokes Company, New York, N.Y., 1913, p. 20; with permission of J. B. Lippincott Company, Philadelphia, Penna.

become familiar with her later studies concerning the prevention of personality disorders in very young children. These studies could be guides for the future; they point the way for world reform through education.

To begin with rediscovery, the outline on the next page has been constructed to indicate the kind of thinking and coordinated sequences that went into Montessori's training procedures. The reasons for presenting it are: (1) to emphasize that mental concepts were built in her pupils by a carefully constructed sequence of experience which proceeded from concrete to abstract, and (2) to show that mental concepts for the language arts and verbal skills were developed by the same process— that is, from concrete experience to abstract. Experience was gained through the "prepared environment" by way of the specially constructed materials.[3] By the proper use of these materials the child taught himself.

To begin with, training was given to one sense at a time. One aim of training the senses individually was to help the child in gaining abstract ideas through his use of materials. By isolating one sense, his mind could give attention to a particular quality. For instance, the color tablets were the same size, weight, and shape, but they differed in the quality of color. In this way he could concentrate on color only, and learn to discriminate among the eight chromatic gradations of eight different colors. Other materials were carefully devised to center his attention on the quality of size, weight, length, width, height, texture, and geometric shapes (square, circle, triangle, trapezium, pentagon, hexagon, septagon, octagon, etc.).

Another reason for exercising the senses one at a time was not to heap new impressions on the young child, but rather to help him create mental order out of all the conglomerate and confusing impressions flowing into him.

Following exercise of the individual senses, the child was helped to combine the naming of the quality (i.e., thick, thin, long, short, etc.)

---

3. E. M. Standing, Maria Montessori: Her Life and Work, Hollis & Carter, Ltd., London, 1957, p. 243.

114

OUTLINE: FROM CONCRETE TO ABSTRACT EXPERIENCE [4]

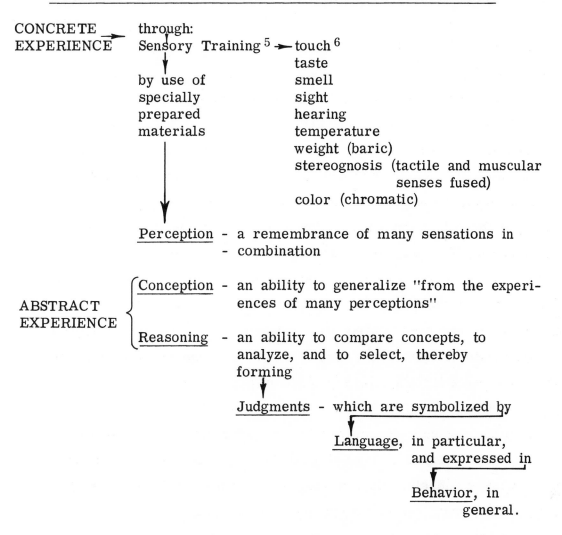

CONCRETE EXPERIENCE → through:

Sensory Training [5] → touch [6]
                taste

by use of specially prepared materials
                smell
                sight
                hearing
                temperature
                weight (baric)
                stereognosis (tactile and muscular senses fused)
                color (chromatic)

Perception - a remembrance of many sensations in
- combination

ABSTRACT EXPERIENCE

Conception - an ability to generalize "from the experiences of many perceptions"

Reasoning - an ability to compare concepts, to analyze, and to select, thereby forming

Judgments - which are symbolized by

Language, in particular, and expressed in

Behavior, in general.

---

4. For the most part, this material was abstracted from Ellen Yale Stevens, A Guide to the Montessori Method, Frederick A. Stokes Company, New York, N.Y., 1913, pp. 74, 112-113.

5. In order to aid the formation of multiple associations, Montessori stressed the training of touch (especially tactile at first), sight, and hearing. The senses were trained individually and in combination by use of materials selected and designed for this purpose.

6. Generally, "up to the age of six, children need to have their vision reinforced by touch if, without great mental fatigue, they are to get an accurate conception of the objects about them."

The "natural way for little ones to learn about things is to touch them." Dorothy Canfield Fisher, A Montessori Mother, Henry Holt and Company, New York, N.Y., 1912, pp. 57-58; with the permission of Holt, Rinehart and Winston, Inc., New York, N.Y.

of each material while handling it. It was by practicing the sensory exercise first, however, that he gained the mental experience and concept of a particular quality.[7] [8] (Refer to the lesson in action in Stevens or Montessori.)

In describing this training of the senses through especially designed materials, there is a point to be made. By some, these materials have been thought of as limited, as not offering creative opportunities for children, as better suited, perhaps, to cultures less cluttered materially—the Latin or the Asian, for example. But if natural development is considered, if the establishment of order in a confused environment is the goal, if putting likes with likes, and if learning to distinguish among many impressions is fostered through methodical self-education, the resulting mental order in the child is preparation for work of increasing complexity—as has been proved over and over in Montessori schools.[9]

Materials designed for a particular purpose and to be used for this purpose only—not for play—have a place in our culture, where many children are overstimulated and sometimes confused.

In preparing children for development of reading and writing skills, mental concepts were developed through the experience of handling concrete language symbols. Handling the symbols preceded the abstract experience of visual recognition of the printed word.

To make a very abbreviated explanation of this training—the language symbols to be handled were the letters, made from rough-feeling material, usually sandpaper, in either script or cursive form, depending on the customary usage of the country. The children simultaneously

---

7. Ellen Yale Stevens, A Guide to the Montessori Method, Frederick A. Stokes Company, New York, N.Y., 1913, pp. 83-88.
8. Maria Montessori, The Montessori Method, Frederick A. Stokes Company, New York, N.Y., 1912, pp. 177-178.
9. "The central idea of the Montessori system, on which every smallest bit of apparatus, every detail of technic rests solidly, is a full recognition of the fact that no human being can be educated by anyone else. He must do it himself or it is never done. And this is as true at the age of three as at the age of thirty . . ." Dorothy Canfield Fisher, A Montessori Mother, Henry Holt and Company, New York, N.Y., 1912, p. 49; with the permission of Holt, Rinehart and Winston, Inc., New York, N.Y.

looked at and handled the movable alphabet (visual, tactile, and kinesthetic experience). Simultaneously, too, they associated the symbols by
saying both name and sound (articulatory and auditory experience). They
also arranged the letters to spell out words.

Time after time, in Montessori school experiments in different
parts of the world, very young children using preparatory concrete language experience of this sort "burst spontaneously into writing" without
ever having written before.[10] They had been able, in a way natural to
them—through concrete sensory-motor experience—to build a mental concept of words as language symbols.

What distinguishes this sensory-motor experience of Montessori's
from any other is the manipulation of actual letters—a step beyond even
Fernald's tracing technique. This manipulation—the using of the letters
to build words—is the child's key to writing. Spoken language is learned
naturally; written language also should come naturally. When the native
inclination to touch, to feel, to move, is put to work in actual handling
of the language symbols (the letters), the ultimate result is growth and
competence in written language skills.[11] Montessori brought the world
of direct experience to the abstract world of the printed page. By employing touch with movement first, by incorporating and associating them
with sight, sound, and articulation, she put biological and developmental
sequence to work in a unified way in achieving the skills in written language growth.

Could not these careful sequences developed by Montessori be adapted to our own culture?[12] Many of the practices, many of the materials
(to which we could add) would be worth trying. They all—sequences,
practices, and materials—should be among the means of solving language

---

10. A quotation used by E. M. Standing in Maria Montessori: Her Life and
Work, Hollis & Carter, Ltd., London, 1957, p. 28.
11. For psychomotor development in the pre-school child see Mussen and
Conger, Child Development and Personality, Harper & Brothers, New York, N.Y.,
1956, pp. 219-220.
12. See "The Joy of Learning," Time, Vol. LXXVII, No. 20, May 12, 1961,
pp. 63-64.

and learning problems early. They should open ways to help the child work toward an integrated personality.

It is in the interest of the integrated personality that we undertake next the discovery of Montessori.

Discovery means boring in to understand the philosophy behind her methods. One of her major principles was the right of the child to freedom—an essential to his development.

It is important to know that in the Montessori schools freedom means "conquest and mastery over oneself."[13] Freedom is not to be interpreted as giving the child license to do anything he chooses, regardless of others. It does not mean he is permitted to come to school dirty, to spend all his time in "play," to abuse his neighbor, to use unfitting language, to destroy materials, etc. It does mean growing up in an environment in which the conditions and the materials assist him to teach and to develop himself. It does mean non-interference from adults when his activity is bringing about development. If he is pouring water from one container into another to learn to make judgments of quantity, the teacher "takes" the mess. If he is throwing water about and disturbing others, she does not "take" the mess.[14] Sally, in chapter iii, was not flipping the pennies; she was gaining number concepts, practicing concentration—in a word, teaching herself. Although she was nine years old, she worked with the pennies for an hour at a time. Obviously, she needed that time and that opportunity for that particular development.

Freedom is a complex thing, requiring help from the environment and carefully given direction from adults—but not severity, not over-gratification, and not laissez-faire. Thus, the Montessori child becomes free because he builds his own inner disciplines through activity in an environment of freedom. He is as happy when he is working and learning as when he is playing.

13. Montessori 1905-1907, Association Montessori Internationale, Amsterdam, 1957, p. 5.
14. Edna Andriano, Montessori trained, who provided, also, the following material: "Some Problems of Education: The Problem of Freedom," Correspondence Courses in the Montessori Method of Education, St. Nicholas' Training Centre for the Montessori Method of Education, 15 Dawson Place, London W2 (Lecture 13).

It is inspiring to read accounts written in the early part of the century by visitors who traveled from different parts of the world to observe the first Montessori schools—Le Case dei Bambini (The Houses of Children). Their amazement at the way in which self-motivated little children were working freely in complete absorption and exercising their own responsible controls, radiates through the pages of these accounts even today, nearly fifty years later.[15] Astonishing results with children in many countries were obtained not only by Dr. Montessori, but also by the trained teachers who have carried on her work.

Discovery of Montessori is more than insight into her concept of freedom; discovery involves some comprehension for her vision and her part in a great social movement.

E. M. Standing puts it very well:

> The century in which we live—and Montessori lived—has been called "The Century of the Child" . . . in no previous epoch in history have there come into existence so many organizations all having as their aim some aspect of the welfare of the child.
> . . . With the extraordinary sensitiveness of genius she [Montessori] was able to discern beneath these manifold expressions the stirring of something deeper—of a great new movement struggling to come to birth from the subconsciousness of the human race.
> As long ago as 1926 Dr. Montessori [said:] "Humanity today. . . resembles an abandoned child who finds himself lost in a wood at night . . . Men do not clearly realize what are the forces that draw them into war, and for that reason they are defenseless against them."
> There must be something radically wrong with our civilization that it should be threatened in this way from within. The vast majority of human beings on this planet do not want war; yet wars come. The causes of war, she would have us believe, are not those which appear on the surface and immediately precipitate its outbreak. They lie deep down in the collective subconscious of humanity.
> The real reason--according to Montessori--is that something was wanting in the building-up of our civilization. A vital factor has been left out: and that is the child as a creative social factor. [Hitherto] we have only taken into account "adult values of life": the child has never been given his rightful place.
> Hitherto we have regarded childhood merely as a stage through which the individual has to pass in order to become an adult, and only of value from the individual's point of view. But childhood is

---

15. For one such account see Dorothy Canfield Fisher, A Montessori Mother, Henry Holt and Company, New York, N.Y., 1912.

more than this. It is an entity in itself with an importance of its own. . . .

Hitherto the child has never been able to fulfill his potentialities, to construct a harmoniously developed adult society.[16]

It was Montessori's purpose to work for the closing of the gap between social behavior and technological advance. For her the hope for the future was the child. Over the past fifty years tremendous progress has been made in the treatment of children. What remains to be done now is to continue the search for laws governing child growth and development from birth on. In the process of discovery, the searcher must observe the child with love; there must be sensitivity for the conditions that are right for the child.[17] It was Montessori's conviction that when the science of his growth and development is fully known, and when the nature of his psyche[18] is understood and respected, then will the race produce a new culture—one in which understanding will replace conflict between child and adult, one in which man will not rush headlong into universal annihilation.[19]

How much Montessori offers our times is the essence of Grisoni's tribute which declares that many principles basic to Dr. Montessori's work are "supremely to the point today. Stress is laid upon them by even very recent research which . . . formulates problems that Maria

---

16. E. M. Standing, Maria Montessori: Her Life and Work, Hollis & Carter, Ltd., London, 1957, pp. 60-62.

17. "This was what education ought to be: an education which started from birth and which was based upon the knowledge of the psychology of human growth: an education which aimed at giving the means and creating the conditions required for the development of man himself." (From a review of Dr. Montessori's address at the time of becoming an Honorary Fellow of the Educational Institute of Scotland, "Education for A New World," The Scottish Educational Journal, Vol. XXIX, No.46, Nov. 15, 1946, p. 642.)

18. "The carrier of . . . consciousness is the individual, who does not produce the psyche on his own volition but is, on the contrary, preformed by it and nourished by the gradual awakening of consciousness during childhood. If the psyche must be granted an overriding empirical importance, so also must the individual, who is the only immediate manifestation of the psyche." C. G. Jung, The Undiscovered Self, Little, Brown and Company, Boston, Mass., 1958, p. 47.

19. Related ideas are reflected by present-day thinkers. For example, Jung in his concern for the individual believes there is much "at stake" in our age of technology and science, and that "so much depends on the psychological constitution of modern man." Ibid., p. 111.

Montessori had stated and widely discussed at a time when the assess-
ments of Neuro-Psychology and Psycho-physiology, which now confirm
them, did not yet exist!"[20]

---

20. Adelaide Colli Grisoni, Professor of Child Neuro-Psychiatry, University
of Milan, as quoted in Montessori 1907-1957, Association Montessori Internationale,
Amsterdam, 1957, p. 3.

CHAPTER VI

SUMMARY AND EVALUATION

What Has Been Said?

A look at the preceding chapters of this book explains the importance of the teacher's planning and working in terms of joint neurophysiological and psychological functioning—of traveling these two roads concurrently.

Although major conclusions would be presumptuous, examples of principles to consider, of techniques, of materials--for individuals, for small groups, for larger groups--all have been suggested here, either through personal experience or that of others.

Attention has been directed to discovery of specific language disability children, a particular category of intelligent children who are scarcely recognized, commonly ignored, or classed with the maladjusted. The loss to society includes the loss of gifted minds.[1]

Actual teaching experience shows that learning is facilitated and even made possible by the use of the sensory-motor avenues simultaneously, or in other associated relationships. Among specific language disability children these related sensory-motor approaches are necessary if reading, spelling, or perhaps writing are to be effective; but because the masses of children in the ordinary classroom have diverse individual imageries, the public school, especially, should benefit from wide and persistent adaptation of carefully planned simultaneous and interrelated

---

1. "The most important thing is for all teachers, psychologists, and doctors to realize the existence of these problems and their considerable dimensions." Knud Hermann, M.D., Reading Disability, Charles C Thomas, Springfield, Ill., 1959, p. 178 (with the permission of the original publisher, Munksgaard A/S, Copenhagen).

sensory-motor approaches for both concrete and verbal learnings.

The suggestion has been made that the above principle serve as a criterion for lesson planning; illustrative problems of individual children have been described; and eminent experimenters have been introduced to give some idea of opening frontiers in psychological, neurophysiological, and educational areas.

How Can We Answer These Questions?

If a neurophysiological approach is to be accepted, what kinds of questions may arise for the classroom teacher? Here are some.

How can training institutions contribute toward preparing the teacher for a neurophysiological teaching approach?

How can administration provide practical support for this approach? By what means can it help teachers to diagnose, to sort out, and to group categories such as:

(a) Specific language disability children

(b) Disturbed children with learning disabilities

(c) Slow children, including slow bloomers

(d) Slow children, including those with difficulties which result from frequent absence, or previous inadequate teaching

(e) Children with vision and hearing defects

Is the teacher prepared to evaluate and choose from among a wide range of methods, materials, and teaching techniques that will be useful to him in his situation? Does he recognize the different types of imagery? Do his teaching plans provide for simultaneous or interrelated use of sensory-motor experience? Would a method fulfilling these requirements for whole classes (such as the Unified Phonics Method by Spalding, for example) be a good choice? If Fernald spelling techniques are to be used, what kinds of graphs or records will be kept to tabulate progress? Where can he obtain training in Gillingham techniques?[2] What among the infinite possibilities of the arts are being tried?

---

2. A beginning in specific language disability training has been made in this country. Hood College, Frederick, Md., has a course under Margaret Rawson, and

How may the classroom teacher who applies sensory-motor approaches in all relationships evaluate his work? Is there a decrease in class failures and a decrease in behavior problems? Is the pupil growing under a plan of self evaluation? Does he have specific goals to work for? Does he know his own strengths and weaknesses? Does he have some type of individual progress chart, i.e., something in which he can participate himself—"the practical aspect of idealism"?

With these thoughts, this chapter concludes a presentation which takes into account the great variety of ways children learn. It is meant to be helpful to anyone interested in education, but to teachers and parents in particular.

Seattle Pacific College, Seattle, Wash., offers a summer course under Mrs. John Slingerland. Examples of public schools where Gillingham techniques and materials have flourished successfully under trained teachers are the Lincoln Public Schools, Lincoln, Mass.; Wayland Public Schools, Wayland, Mass.; Peterborough Public Schools, Peterborough, N.H.; and Renton Public Schools, Renton, Wash. Examples of private schools include the following: Ethical Culture Midtown School, New York, N.Y.; Fieldston Lower School, New York, N.Y.; Hawken School, Cleveland, Ohio; Francis W. Parker School, Chicago, Ill.; Barstow School, Kansas City, Mo.; St. Martin's Protestant Episcopal School, New Orleans, La.; and the Oakwood School, North Hollywood, Calif. (See Bulletin of the Orton Society, The Orton Society, Inc., Vol. XI, May, 1961.) In addition, Mrs. Helene Durbrow, consultant, Camp Mansfield, Underhill Center, Vt., trains teachers and works out programs for both private and public schools; The Language Training Center at The Children's Hospital Medical Center, Boston, Mass., trains tutors; and Massachusetts General Hospital Language Clinic, Boston, Mass., has a program for teachers.

In Denmark, word-blindness is a recognized condition, and Copenhagen has a center (the Word-Blind Institute) where language disability is studied and training for teachers is given.

1966 Postscript:
(a) Among other persons who have long provided experienced training resources are: Sally B. Childs, Dallas Language Research and Training Program, The Hockaday School, 11600 Welch Road, Dallas, Tex.; and June Lyday Orton, the Orton Reading Center, Winston-Salem, N.C.

(b) Mrs. Slingerland has expanded her teacher training activities to such public schools as the Highland Park Independent School District and the Richardson Independent School District of Dallas, Tex.

(c) In the same city (Dallas) there is a teacher training group at the Scottish Rite Hospital for Crippled Children under Dr. Lucius Waites, Neurological Division.

(d) Well-established language centers for diagnoisis, teaching, and research usually have been located in the large cities. Examples are: Pediatric Language Disorder Clinic, Columbia-Presbyterian Medical Center, New York City; the Albany Study Center for Learning Disabilities, State University of New York at Albany and Albany Medical College. By contrast, a new development is the setting up of a center for the non-metropolitan community. One of these is the Perceptual Education and Research Center, Sherborn, Mass.

(e) Schools and clinics with intensive programs for dyslexics are on the in-

What Is The Outlook?

It does seem certain that the concerns of our time demand total effort—physical, intellectual, spiritual. Only total effort can gain for America the destiny Emerson saw—"a new and more excellent social state than history has recorded."[3]

And so, in matters of selecting and training quality students, of improving the caliber of mass education, and of sharing in some areas of personal counseling, teachers have vital tasks to be fulfilled with children and their programs. In my opinion, these tasks add up to powerful reasons for believing that every teacher today, regardless of his assignment, has responsibility, _primary_ responsibility, for participating in educational guidance—which in this book has meant planning learning programs for all types of intelligent children in all sorts of situations.

---

crease. Examples of two experienced facilities are: the summer school at Freyburg Academy Reading Research Institute, Freyburg, Me.; the DeWitt Reading Clinic, San Rafael, Calif.

(f) Total reading programs (providing preventive, developmental, corrective, and remedial services) have been undertaken where school populations border on the enormous--a courageous and gargantuan pioneer task. Baltimore County, Md., is a notable example.

(g) The Montessori explosion is truly important-if the depth of Montessori's ideas is not sacrificed in the race for techniques and materials.

(h) The passage of such laws as California's A.B. 464, which authorizes programs for educationally handicapped minors, opens up possibilities for still more assistance and understanding for the individual child and his problems.

(i) Although much understanding is yet to be gained, interest and activity in rescuing the dyslexic child is mushrooming. The real roadblock everwhere is the lack of teacher training.

3. Newton Dillaway (editor), _The Gospel of Emerson_, The Montrose Press, Wakefield, Mass., 1949, p. 1.